COMPLETE GUIDE
to the
TOEFL® Test, CBT Edition

Answer Key and Tapescipt

BRUCE ROGERS
Economics Institute

HEINLE & HEINLE

THOMSON LEARNING

United States • Canada • Mexico • Singapore • Spain • United Kingdom

HEINLE & HEINLE

THOMSON LEARNING

Heinle & Heinle's Complete Guide to the TOEFL® Test, CBT Edition
Answer Key and Tapescript
Bruce Rogers

Publisher: Nancy Leonhardt
Production Editor: Sarah Cogliano
Marketing Managers: Charlotte Sturdy, Amy Mabley
Manufacturing Coordinator: Marybeth Hennebury

Composition/Interior Design: Roberta J. Landi Book Production
Cover Design: Julie Gecha
Printer: Mazer Corporation

ISBN: 0-8384-1232-7

International Division List

ASIA (excluding India)
Thomson Learning
60 Albert Street #15-01
Albert Complex
Singapore 189969

AUSTRALIA/NEW ZEALAND
Nelson/Thomson Learning
102 Dodds Street
South Melbourne
Victoria 3205 Australia

CANADA
Nelson/Thomson Learning
1120 Birchmount Road
Scarborough, Ontario
Canada M1K 5G4

LATIN AMERICA
Thomson Learning
Seneca, 53
Colonia Polanco
11560 México D.F. México

SPAIN
Thomson Learning
Calle Magallanes, 25
28015-Madrid
Espana

UK/EUROPE/MIDDLE EAST
Thomson Learning
Berkshire House
168-173 High Holborn
London, WC1V 7AA, United Kingdom

Table of Contents

Section 3: Reading

Table of Contents

Section 4: Essay Writing

Practice Tests

Section 1: Listening

Preview Test 1: Listening

Answer Key

Part A

 1. Someone painted it.
 2. Go to his car.
 3. He doesn't have to read all the books.
 4. Using the software is simple.
 5. When to meet his brother.
 6. His letter arrived unexpectedly.
 7. He rarely changes his grades.
 8. He shouldn't drop the class.
 9. She put a list of grades on the door.
10. He doesn't take responsibility for errors.
11. An identification card.
12. He got on the wrong bus.
13. The board will not choose a dean this month.
14. They wish they hadn't paid attention to Harvey.
15. A hotel room.
16. Some students are not on his list.
17. The match wouldn't be played.

Part B

18. Mathematics.
19. Get a tutor.
20. Encouraging.
21. They are about the same size. / They are relatively close together.
22. The phases of Venus.
23. That it was not a single object but two objects. / That there was life beneath its cloud cover.
24. It is longer than a Venus year.
25. (A), (D), (B), (C)
26. The Earth.
27. To pay for everyday expenses.
28. Selling gifts at a museum.
29. Fill out some forms.
30. Eighteenth and nineteenth century music in the United States.

31. It has a long history. / It appeared in the *Bay Psalm Book*.
32. (B)
33. (A)
34. (A), (C), (B)
35. His songs show a variety of influences.
36. The students' final project.
37. Having the subjects flip coins. / Using a computer program that makes random choices.
38. Their grade performance will not be affected by exercise.
39. (D),(C), (A), (B)
40. On the last day of class.

Audio Script

Part A

1. **F1:** I like your new bicycle, Henry.
   M1: Thanks, but it isn't new. I had my old one repainted.
   M2: What can be said about Henry's bicycle?

2. **F2:** Will that be cash, check, or charge?
   M1: I'm going to write a check, but I just realized I left my checkbook in my car. I'll be right back.
   M2: What will the man probably do next?

3. **M1:** I'll never be able to get through all these books on Professor Bryant's reading list.
   F2: But Mark, not all of them are required.
   M2: What does the woman tell Mark?

4. **M1:** What do you think of the new software?
   F1: It's really easy to use.
   M1: Isn't it though!
   M2: What does the man mean?

5. **M1:** Anyone call while I was gone?
   F1: Your brother did. He wants you to meet him for dinner.
   M1: Oh, really? Did he say what time?
   M2: What does the man want to know?

6. **F2:** Have you heard from Howard lately?
   M1: Funny you should ask. Yesterday, from out of the blue, I got a letter from him.
   M2: What does the man say about Howard?

7. **M1:** I think I deserved a higher grade in chemistry class. Does Professor Welch ever change the grades he gives?
   F1: Sure—about once a century!
   M2: What can be inferred about Professor Welch from this conversation?

Section 1: Listening

8. **M1:** I'm going to drop my political science class. It meets too early in the morning for me.

   F2: Allen, is that *really* a good reason to drop the class?

   M2: What is the woman really saying to Allen?

9. **M1:** How did you do on Professor Porter's test?

   F1: I have no idea—she hasn't returned them yet.

   M1: No, but she's posted the grades on her office door.

   M2: What does the man say about Professor Porter?

10. **F1:** William comes up with some weak excuse or another for just about every mistake he makes, doesn't he?

    F2: Wait till you hear his latest!

    M2: What do the speakers imply about William?

11. **F1:** Did your student ID card ever turn up?

    M1: Yeah, the manager of the campus bookstore called me yesterday and said it was there. I guess I took it out when I cashed a check and didn't put it back in my wallet.

    F1: Well, you're lucky you got it back.

    M1: I know. I'm going to have to take better care of it in the future.

    M2: What did the man think he had lost?

12. **F2:** We should be arriving at the airport in another ten minutes.

    M1: Wait a second—this bus is going to the *airport*?

    M2: What can be inferred about the man?

13. **M1:** I wonder when the board of regents will pick a new dean.

    F1: Who knows? They're not even scheduled to meet until next month.

    M2: What does the woman imply?

14. **M1:** We should never have listened to Harvey.

    F1: If only we'd asked someone else for advice!

    M2: What do they mean?

15. **M2:** How was your room last night?

    M1: I slept like a baby. And the rates were quite reasonable.

    M2: What are the men probably discussing?

16. **M1:** All right, let's begin by taking a quick look at the syllabus I just handed out.

    F1: Uh, Professor White? A few of us in the back of the room didn't get a copy of it.

    M1: Hmm . . . there are 23 names on my class list, so I only brought 23 copies.

    M2: What can be inferred from Professor White's remark?

17. **F2:** Peter is favored to win the tennis match Saturday.

    M1: Oh, then that match wasn't canceled after all?

    M2: What had the man *originally* assumed?

Part B

Questions 18–20

M1: (*knock, knock*) Hi, Professor Lamont. May I come in?

F1: Oh, hi, Scott, sure. What's on your mind?

M1: Well, I've decided I should drop my advanced math course.

F1: Hmm, you're majoring in biochemistry, right? Well, that's a required course for your major.

M1: I know. But maybe I could take it next semester.

F1: Besides, to do well in biochemistry, you need to know math. Math is the language of science.

M1: I know—my father always says trying to study science without knowing math is like trying to study music without knowing how to read notes.

F1: Well, your father is absolutely right.

M1: But I've gotten really low grades on the first two quizzes. Maybe I should just change majors.

F1: I wouldn't do that if I were you, Scott. Why don't you try to get a graduate student to tutor you, and see if you can pull your grades up? I think you can do it.

18. What course does Scott want to drop?
19. What does Professor Lamont suggest that Scott do?
20. Which of the following best describes Professor Lamont's attitude towards Scott?

Questions 21–26

M2: Listen to a student's presentation in an astronomy class. Students in the class are giving presentations on our Solar System. This presentation focuses on the planet Venus.

M1: Well, uh, hi, everyone . . . Monday we heard Don tell us about the Sun and Lisa talk about Mercury, the planet closest to the Sun. My report today is about the next planet, Venus. Okay, now you may already know that, except for the Moon and Sun, Venus is the brightest object in the sky. You can see it in the morning and in the evening. In fact, a long time ago, people thought that Venus was two distinct objects: Phosphorus, the morning star, and Hesperus, the evening star. Oh, and when you look at Venus with a telescope, you can actually see the "phases" of Venus—just like the phases of the Moon. That's because different parts of Venus' sunlit area face Earth at different times.

One of the articles I read about Venus said that sometimes it's called "Earth's twin." That's because Venus and Earth are just about the same size, and also because they are so close together. Only Earth's moon gets closer to Earth than Venus does. But, from what I learned, Earth and Venus are not really that much alike. For a long time people didn't know much of anything about Venus because it's covered with clouds, which are mainly made of carbon dioxide and sulfur dioxide—and uh—some other gases, too. People used to think that under the clouds there might be strange jungles full of alien monsters. But nowadays we know Venus is way too hot for that—hotter than an oven! It's too hot even to have liquid water, so—no jungles! No monsters!

Here's a strange fact about Venus. It takes Venus only 225 Earth days to go around the sun, as opposed to Earth which takes 365 days, of course—that's what we call a year. But Venus spins around on its axis really slowly. It takes about 243 Earth days to spin around completely. The Earth takes—you guessed it . . . 24 hours. That means that a day on Venus is longer than a year on Venus! And here's something else weird—

Venus doesn't rotate in the same direction as any of the other planets. It has what they call a, uh—let's see, a "retrograde" spin.

Now, there have been a lot of space probes that have gone to Venus, so I'll only mention some of the most important ones. There's one there now called Magellan that is making incredibly detailed maps of the surface by using radar. It's been there since 1990. The first probe to go there was Mariner 2. That was back in 1962. Another important one was the Venera 4, which was a Soviet space probe. It arrived there in—let's see—1967 and dropped instruments onto the surface with a parachute. Then there was the Venus Pioneer 2, in 1978. It entered the atmosphere and found out the atmosphere was made mainly of carbon dioxide. As I said, there were a lot of other ones too.

Well, uh, that's about all I have to say about Venus, unless you have some questions. Caroline will be giving the next report, which is about the third planet from the Sun. Since we all live there, that one should be pretty interesting!

21. According to the speaker, in what ways are Earth and Venus twins?
22. Which of the following can be seen through a telescope aimed at Venus?
23. According to the speaker, which of the following were once common beliefs about the planet Venus?
24. Which of the following does the speaker say about the length of a day on Venus?
25. In what order were these space probes sent to Venus?
26. It can be inferred that the topic of the next student's presentation will be which of the following?

Questions 27–29

M2: Listen to a telephone conversation:

(*Ring, ring. . . .*)

F2: Hello, Financial Aid Office. Connie Wilson speaking.

F1: Hello, Ms. Wilson. My name is Dana Hart. I was calling to get some information about the work-study program.

F2: I'll be happy to tell you about it. What would you like to know?

F1: Well, I've got a bank loan to pay for my tuition, and my parents are helping me out with my room-and-board expenses, but I just don't have much for spending money.

F2: It sounds like work-study might be perfect for you, then.

F1: What sort of jobs are available right now? I don't want to work in a cafeteria. Are there any openings at the art gallery in the Student Union?

F2: Let me check. (*Sound of keystrokes on computer. . . .*) No, no openings there. But there is a position at the university museum, working in the gift shop.

F1: Hmm, I think I might enjoy doing that. What do I have to do to apply for this job?

F2: Well, the first step is to come down to the Financial Aid Office to fill out a couple of forms. You can get them from the receptionist at the front desk. Then I'll call and set up an interview for you with Dr. Ferrarra. He's the personnel director at the museum. Dr. Ferrarra has to approve you for the position.

F1: OK, well, thanks a lot for all the information. I'll try to stop by either this afternoon or tomorrow.

27. Why does Dana want to find a job?

28. What job is Dana probably going to apply for?

29. What must Dana do first to apply for the job she is interested in?

Questions 30–35

M2: Listen to a lecture in a music class.

M1: Does anyone know what the first book to be published in the British colonies in North America was? (*Pause . . .*) No? Well, it was a book of religious music, called the B*ay Psalm Book.* It contained 13 tunes, some of which, such as "Old Hundred," are still sung today. Then, after about 1750, native-born musicians in New England began to write their own songs, and they were pretty strange songs, too, by the standards of the day. With their angular melodies and open-fifth chords, they were considered quite unusual by Europeans.

Now, after a while, traditional New England religious music migrated South and evolved into what we call Southern revival hymns. These songs include some standards, such as "Amazing Grace" and "Wayfaring Stranger." Most of them were livelier than the New England songs. Southern revival hymns were typically printed in "shape notes," an easy-to-read system of notation. In this system, the notes appear in the form of geometric shapes to represent the notes of the scale.

Another popular form of music in the nineteenth century, especially in the South, was the minstrel song. It was usually performed by a four-man troupe who performed on the banjo, tambourine, castanets, and fiddle. Decatur Emmet was the most famous composer of minstrel songs. His best known work today is probably the song "Dixie."

Then there were parlor songs. Parlor songs were very sentimental songs, usually about ordinary aspects of domestic life. One example is "The Old Arm Chair," written in 1840 by Henry Russell, an English singer who toured the United States in the 1830s and 40s.

The greatest songwriter of the early nineteenth century, in my opinion, was Stephen Foster, who composed songs for the famous Christy Minstrels, such as "Oh, Susanna" and "Camptown Races" and parlor songs such as "Beautiful Dreamer." His songs are still popular today. His melodies were simple, much like traditional folk melodies, and he combined elements of English, Irish, and African-American music with Italian operatic tunes to create some immortal songs.

Well, I'm going to stop talking and give you all a chance to hear some of the music from the late 18th and early 19th centuries. First, there will be a couple of traditional religious tunes from New England, then some Southern revival hymns. After that, we'll hear some minstrel songs and some parlor songs, and a medley of songs by Stephen Foster.

30. What is the main topic of this lecture?

31. What does the speaker indicate about the song "Old Hundred"?

32. Which of these is the best representation of the notational system used for Southern revival hymns?

33. Which of these instruments was typically used to play minstrel songs?

34. Match the song with the correct musical category.

35. What does the speaker say about Stephen Foster?

Questions 36–40

F1: Listen to a discussion involving an assignment in a psychology class:

M1: Class, today I'm going to talk about the final project for this class, which is to design and conduct your own psychological experiment.

M2: Is this in place of the final exam?

M1: No, it's in addition to it. However, you won't have to do a research paper in this class—just the final exam and this experiment. It's not due until the last day of the semester.

M3: Professor Hunter, could you tell us a little more about how to go about this?

M1: Yes, of course. As you'll learn from reading Chapter 2, a psychological experiment, like any experiment, begins with . . . anyone know? Tom?

M3: With a hypothesis?

M1: And what is a hypothesis, Tom?

M3: Well, it's a theory . . . an assumption that you try to prove in your experiment.

M1: Good definition. Now, the most basic psychological experiment consists of a number of subjects divided into a control group and an experimental group. What's the difference between these two groups? Raymond, do you know?

M2: Well, I think that, during the experiment, the conditions for the two groups have to be exactly the same except for one factor, right? So the experimental group is exposed to this factor, and the control group isn't.

M1: Uh huh, and we call that factor, whatever it is, the independent variable. If there is some measurable change in the behavior of the experimental group, then the experiment indicates that the independent variable may have been the cause of the change. And that change in behavior is called the dependent variable. Yes, Tom, you have a question?

M3: Yeah, okay, suppose I want to do an experiment to prove that students who exercise every day get better grades . . .

M1: Okay, that would be your hypothesis then—that daily exercise affects grade performance . . .

M3: So I divide up my subjects into two groups . . .

M1: Well, you'll want to figure out a way to randomly divide the subjects into two groups.

M2: Why is that?

M1: To avoid bias and keep the experiment as objective as possible. If you let the subjects divide themselves into a group, then people with the same interests and inclinations tend to form groups. If you do it yourself, then you may put certain people into certain groups to influence the outcome of the experiment.

M2: So, I get one group to agree to exercise every day for an hour or more, say, and I get the other group to agree not to do any special exercise.

M1: Good. Let's draw a simplified diagram of this experiment on the board . . . what would be the independent variable?

M3: Exercise, I suppose.

M1: Yes, and the dependent variable would be . . . what?

M3: Better grades, right?

M1: Precisely. This has the potential to be a very interesting experiment. You have a question?

M2: Professor, when did you say this project is due?

M1: Well, by sometime next week, I'd like you to submit a basic hypothesis and a summary of how you intend to test it. I'll need to approve that before you go on. Then, by October, you should complete a detailed design for your experiment and recruit subjects if you are going to be working with human subjects. By November, you should complete the experiment itself and start working on an analysis of the data and write up a conclusion. You'll need to submit a complete report on your experiment by the end of the term.

M3: You mean on the final exam day?

M1: No, on the last day of actual classes. I'll read over your reports and give you a grade and return them to you by the day of the final exam. Any other questions?

36. What is the main topic of this discussion?
37. It can be inferred that Professor Hunter would approve of which of these methods of selecting subjects for groups?
38. In the experiment proposed by the student, what can be inferred about the people in the control group?
39. In what order should the students complete these tasks?
40. When is the completed project due?

Listening Part A: Dialogues

Exercise 1.1

Answer Key

1. B	4. A	7. A	10. A	13. B
2. B	5. A	8. A	11. B	14. A
3. A	6. B	9. B	12. A	15. B

Audio Script

1. **M1:** I've never had to wait so long just to pay for a few groceries!
   F1: I think you should get in another line.
   M2: What does the woman suggest the man do?

2. **M1:** How did your baby-sitting job go?
   F2: Oh, fine—the children spent most of the day going down the hill on their new sled.
   M2: What did the children do?

3. **M1:** Where should I put these letters for you?
   F1: Just toss them in that file.
   M2: What does the woman tell the man to do with the letters?

4. **F2:** Did you get your suitcase packed?
   M1: Yeah—but now I can't close it!
   M2: What is the man's problem?

5. **F1:** What kind of bread did Annie bake?
    F2: My favorite—whole wheat bread!
    M2: What is learned about Annie's bread?

6. **F1:** Has Brenda finished writing her story for the radio news?
    M1: Oh, sure—she's just taping it now.
    M2: What does the man say about the story?

7. **M1:** Did you know Emily has a new address?
    F1: No, I didn't realize that. Do you have it?
    M1: Yeah, hang on—I wrote it down somewhere.
    M2: What is learned about Emily?

8. **F2:** How's the coffee here, Dennis?
    M1: I think it's a little better these days.
    M2: What does Dennis say about the coffee?

9. **F1:** I bought a ticket for the lottery. I hope I win.
    M1: What's the prize, Ellen?
    M2: What does the man ask Ellen?

10. **M1:** I wonder if this old bottle I found is worth any money. It's a beautiful color.
    F2: Yes, but look—there's a chip in it.
    M2: What does the woman say about the bottle?

11. **F1:** I saw Jerry is walking on crutches.
    M1: Yeah, he had an accident last week.
    F1: Really? What happened?
    M1: His feet slipped in some oil and he twisted his knee.
    M2: What happened to Jerry?

12. **M2:** This is a beautiful part of the state.
    M1: Yes, it certainly is. What's it most famous for?
    M2: Well, you'll see some remarkable race horses here.
    M2: Why is this area well known?

13. **M1:** So, did the Student Council finally reach a decision?
    F2: Finally—after they fought about the issue all afternoon.
    M2: How did the Student Council spend the afternoon?

14. **F1:** I've never seen you in that shirt before.
    M1: I don't wear it very often—it's too tight in the collar.
    M2: What is the problem with the shirt?

15. **F1:** Are you having a mid-term exam in Professor Maguire's class?
    F2: No, he assigned a paper instead.
    M2: What did Professor Maguire do?

Exercise 1.2

Answer Key

1. He wrote her an e-mail.
2. He's unhappy because he lost the election.
3. It deals with life on Earth.
4. They won't leave until the rain is over.
5. He offered his help to Darlene.
6. Eat in the coffee shop.
7. He can lend the man a pen.
8. The flooding in the east part of campus was severe.
9. Correct the exams.
10. The lease is difficult to read.

Audio Script

1. **F1:** Steven, did you ever write a letter to your friend Gloria?
   M1: I sent her an e-mail.
   M2: What is learned about Steven and Gloria?

2. **M1:** I understand that Stuart is going to resign as vice-president.
   F1: As a matter of fact, he's so disappointed that he wasn't elected president, he's quitting the club.
   M2: What does the woman say about Stuart?

3. **F1:** I'm planning to take a class in ecology next term.
   M1: What will you be studying?
   F1: Well, according to the course catalogue, it's the systematic study of life on this planet.
   M1: That sounds interesting.
   M2: What does the woman say about the class she is going to take?

4. **M1:** Are you ready to go now, Janet?
   F1: As soon as the rain stops.
   M2: What does Janet tell the man?

5. **M1:** I heard Darlene was having a hard time with her physics homework.
   F2: Yes, but Sam has kindly offered to assist her.
   M2: What does the woman say about Sam?

6. **F1:** I need to get a quick bite before we go to the workshop.
   M1: There's a coffee shop here in the hotel.
   M2: What does the man suggest the woman do?

7. **M1:** How can I take notes if I don't have anything to write with?
   F2: You can probably borrow a pen from Gus—he always has one behind his ear.
   M2: What does the woman say about Gus?

8. **M2:** Was the flood bad in the east part of campus?

   F1: Bad! We practically needed boats to leave the dormitory!

   M2: What does the woman imply?

9. **M1:** So, Jane, what are your duties as Professor Ramsay's assistant?

   F1: For one thing, I help him correct tests.

   M2: What does Jane help Professor Ramsay do?

10. **F1:** Bonnie, you did look over the lease before you signed it, didn't you?

    F2: Well, I tried to, but not even a lawyer could understand this lease.

    M2: What does Bonnie mean?

Exercise 2.1

Answer Key

1. A	4. A	7. B	10. A
2. B	5. B	8. B	11. B
3. B	6. A	9. B	12. B

Audio Script

1. **M1:** What did you get Suzie for her birthday?

   F2: Didn't you read the invitation to her party? She said she didn't want anyone to bring any presents.

2. **M2:** I've got to go back to the library again after dinner.

   F1: I know you've got a lot of research to do, but don't overdo it. You're spending half your life in the library.

3. **M2:** Did you hear that there was an explosion in the chemistry lab this morning?

   F2: No, was it bad?

   M2: Fortunately, no one was hurt, but it blew out a few panes of glass.

4. **F1:** I can't find my gloves.

   M1: Well, I certainly don't know where they are.

5. **M1:** I looked and looked for a parking place, but there just wasn't one anywhere.

   F2: So what did you do?

   M1: I parked in a loading zone.

   F2: You could have been fined for that!

6. **M1:** You need to fill out a change of address form.

   M2: Oh—is this the right form for that?

7. **M1:** You went to the meeting last night?

   M2: Yes, but I wish I hadn't. Was I ever bored!

8. **M1:** What kind of car are you looking for?
   F1: I don't care, as long as it's dependable. I can't stand a car that breaks down all the time.

9. **M2:** Don't you just love Andrew's boat?
   F2: It's terrific. And it's for sale, you know.

10. **F1:** What a beautiful view of the mountains!
    M1: You're right. I'd like to build a cabin here.
    F1: This would be the perfect site.

11. **F2:** Did you get your garden planted?
    M1: Well, I got a start—I planted a few rows of corn.

12. **F1:** Shh—talking isn't allowed in this part of the library.
    M2: Oh, it's okay to talk in *this* part.

Exercise 2.2

Answer Key

1. A	**3.** A	**5.** A	**7.** A	**9.** B
2. B	**4.** B	**6.** A	**8.** B	**10.** B

Audio Script

1. **F1:** Where have you been keeping yourself, Ben? I haven't seen you since January at least.
   M2: I've had this terrible cold, and I haven't gotten out much.

2. **F2:** What a kind person Glen is.
   M1: Isn't he though!

3. **M1:** Will it be cold in the mountains?
   F1: I'd bring a light sweater if I were you—it may get a little chilly at night.

4. **M2:** Is this where the aeronautics exhibit is going to be?
   F2: No, it'll be in the north wing of the museum.

5. **F1:** Where did you get these statistics?
   M1: In the tables at the back of this book.

6. **M1:** I'm going to paint these old wooden chairs white. They'll look good as new.
   M2: You'd better take off that old coat of red first.

7. **M1:** How do you like your geology class?
   F2: It's an interesting subject—and tomorrow, we're going out into the field to look for fossils.
   M1: Well, good luck—hope you find some!

8. **F1:** There's a movie a movie on television tonight about Abraham Lincoln.
   F2: Who's playing Lincoln?

9. (*Ring . . . Ring . . .*)
   F2: Good afternoon . . . Blue Dolphin Restaurant.
   M2: Yes, this is Mr. Adams. I'd like reservations for eight o'clock Friday evening.
   F2: Fine, Mr. Adams. How many will there be in your party?

10. **F2:** When is your composition class?
    M1: Next period.

Exercise 2.3

Answer Key

1. Look for mistakes.
2. The man's performance in class.
3. This was the first herd he'd ever seen.
4. Follow the directions on the sign.
5. He can't carry the luggage by himself.
6. Put on some other clothes.
7. The class had a better opinion of him.
8. She's sorry that the seminar is over.
9. The park is across the street from the zoo.
10. He doesn't have enough coins.

Audio Script

1. **M1:** I'm ready to hand in my research paper.
   F1: Better check your writing first, Tom.
   M2: What does the woman suggest Tom do?

2. **F2:** How did you do on Dr. Johnson's history exam?
   M1: Well, I passed anyway. But I wish I'd studied more.
   M2: What are they discussing?

3. **M1:** I went to the national park this weekend.
   F2: Did you see the buffaloes?
   M1: Yeah, and you know what? It was the first herd of buffaloes I'd ever seen.
   M2: What does the man mean?

4. **M1:** Which line do I get in if I've already pre-registered?
   F2: Read the sign, why don't you?
   M2: What does the woman tell the man to do?

5. **M2:** Can I leave my luggage here for a couple of hours?

   F2: Sure, you can store it in that room up on the second floor.

   M2: Okay. But I don't think I can handle all these suitcases by myself.

   M2: What does the man mean?

6. **F1:** You're soaked, John. You look like you fell into a swimming pool. What happened?

   M1: I was caught out in a sudden shower.

   F1: Well, you should change your clothes.

   M2: What does the woman think John should do?

7. **F2:** Patrick, what did your classmates think when you won the award?

   M1: Well, it certainly didn't hurt my standing with them.

   M2: What does Patrick mean?

8. **M1:** Is that seminar you were always complaining about finally over?

   F2: Yeah, but you know, now that it's over, I miss going to it.

   M2: What does the woman mean?

9. **F1:** We're going to have the picnic in Pineview Park.

   M1: I don't know where that is.

   F1: It's on Vine Street, right across from the city zoo.

   M2: What does the woman tell the man?

10. **F2:** Why don't you use that pay phone over there to call Cindy?

    M1: Okay, but, ummm . . . do you happen to have more change?

    M2: What is the problem?

Exercise 3.1

Answer Key

1.	A met unexpectedly	6.	B a little sick
2.	A was in trouble	7.	A looks like
3.	B quickly became friends	8.	B Help her
4.	A simple	9.	B isn't far from
5.	B immediately	10.	B didn't like

Audio Script

1. **M2:** I had an interesting conversation with Caroline today.

   F1: Really? Where did you see her?

   M2: I bumped into her in the cafeteria.

   F1: What does the man mean?

2. **M2:** So, Rita, you left work early yesterday?

   F1: Yeah, and did I ever get in hot water for that!

   F2: What does Rita mean?

3. **M1:** I talked to Chuck at the party.
   F1: What did you think of Chuck?
   M1: Oh, we hit it off right away.
   F2: What does the man mean?

4. **M2:** How was the test?
   F1: Piece of cake!
   F2: What does the woman mean?

5. **F1:** Robert, are you ready to leave?
   M1: At the drop of a hat!
   F2: What does Robert imply?

6. **F1:** Julie wasn't at band practice today.
   M2: She's been under the weather lately.
   F2: What does the man imply about Julie?

7. **F1:** There's Albert and his grandfather.
   M1: Wow, Albert really takes after him, doesn't he?
   F2: What does the man say about Albert?

8. **M2:** That suitcase looks heavy, Paula.
   F1: It's heavy, all right. Could you please give me a hand with it?
   F2: What does Paula ask the man to do?

9. **M1:** I just found an apartment on Woodbury Street.
   F1: That's pretty close to campus, isn't it?
   M1: Just a stone's throw away.
   F2: What does the man mean?

10. **M1:** Did you hear Graham's proposal?
    F1: Yes, and I didn't think much of it, to tell the truth.
    F2: What does the woman say about Graham's proposal?

Exercise 3.2

Answer Key

Set A		Set B	
1.	A	11.	B
2.	B	12.	B
3.	A	13.	A
4.	A	14.	B
5.	A	15.	A
6.	B	16.	B
7.	B	17.	A
8.	A	18.	B
9.	B	19.	A
10.	B	20.	A

Audio Script

Set A

1. **F1:** Did you know Max is planning to open his own business? He could make a lot of money.
   M2: Yeah, I suppose—if it ever gets off the ground.
   F2: What does the man mean?

2. **F1:** How long have you had these old tires on your car?
   M2: For over five years. I wonder how much longer they'll last.
   F1: I wouldn't push my luck much further if I were you, Gary.
   F2: What does the woman imply?

3. **F1:** Well, that was a good program. Want to watch something else?
   M1: Not me—I'm ready to turn in.
   F2: What will the man do next?

4. **M1:** Alice, what did you think of that comedian's jokes?
   F1: To tell you the truth, a lot of them went over my head.
   F2: What does Alice mean?

5. **M2:** You look hot and tired. How about some ice water?
   F1: Just what the doctor ordered!
   F2: What does the woman mean?

6. **F1:** Your sister's name is Liz?
   M1: Well, everyone calls her that—it's short for Elizabeth.
   F2: What is learned from this conversation?

7. **M2:** I had lunch at that new restaurant over on College Avenue the other day.
   F1: Oh, I've heard some good things about that place. What did you think of it?
   M2: I'd call it run of the mill.
   F2: What does the man say about the restaurant?

8. **M1:** Just listen to the sound of the creek and the wind in the trees.
   F1: It's like music to my ears!
   F2: What does the woman mean?

9. **M2:** Whew, I'm tired. These boxes of books are heavy.
   F2: Want me to lend a hand?
   F2: What does the woman offer to do?

10. **M2:** Did you see that it was snowing earlier this morning?
    F1: I could hardly believe my eyes! Who ever saw snow here at this time of year?
    F2: What does the woman mean?

Set B

11. **M1:** You've been skiing a lot lately, Karen.
    F1: It really gets in the blood.
    F2: What does Karen mean?

12. **M2:** Norman thinks we don't study enough.
    F1: Look who's talking!
    F2: What does the woman imply about Norman?

13. **M1:** Would you like to go to the West Coast with my friends and me over spring break? We're going to drive out there in my friend Mike's van.
    F1: I'm not sure if I can afford to. Gasoline alone will cost a fortune.
    M1: Not if we all chip in.
    F2: What does the man mean?

14. **M2:** Donna, did you talk to Professor Holmes about that teaching assistantship?
    F1: Yeah, and I didn't even make an appointment. I just marched right into his office and told him why he should choose me!
    M2: Boy, that took a lot of nerve!
    F2: What does the man say about Donna?

15. **F1:** Dan, we still need to paint the kitchen.
    M1: I know, but let's call it a day for now.
    F2: What does Dan mean?

16. **M2:** Let's go over Scene 3 again. I'll get you a script to read from.
    F1: Oh, you don't have to—I've already learned my lines by heart.
    F2: What does the woman mean?

17. **M1:** So Marina, your parents still don't think you should go to Alaska this summer?
    F1: Oh, they'll come around, I think.
    F2: What does Marina think her parents will do?

18. **F1:** Was there someone on your basketball team last year named Rob Martin?
    M1: Rob Martin? Hmmm . . . the name doesn't ring a bell.
    F2: What does the man imply?

19. **M2:** How's your research project coming, Arlene?
    F1: Slowly but surely, it's getting done.
    F2: What does Arlene mean?

20. **M2:** Molly decided to go to graduate school in San Francisco.
    F1: Oh, you must have been sorry to see her leave.
    M2: That goes without saying.
    F2: What does the man imply about Molly?

Exercise 3.3

Answer Key

1. Get some exercise.
2. If the red tie looks good with his shirt.
3. She missed Friday's class, too.
4. He doesn't want to work in a restaurant.
5. He wants to know if the woman is joking.
6. The launch was delayed.
7. Her sweater made her easy to spot.
8. He deserved to get a speeding ticket.
9. He won't be very cooperative.
10. The man didn't get her a watch.
11. In the end, she won't have a problem.
12. He won't be able to take a trip.
13. His father studied medicine.
14. He would be upset if he had lost money.
15. If he has been informed.
16. The cabin is not luxurious.

Audio Script

1. **F1:** Did you finish studying for your chemistry final?
    M1: No, but I'm ready to take a break. Want to go out for coffee?
    F1: Maybe later. Right now, I'm going to go work out at the gym.
    F2: What is the woman going to do next?

2. **F1:** The party is starting soon. Aren't you ready yet?
    M2: I just have to decide on a tie. Do you think this red one goes with my shirt?
    F2: What does the man want to know?

3. **M1:** Do you have notes from Professor Morrison's psychology class Friday? I missed class that day.
    F1: Guess we're in the same boat!
    F2: What does the woman imply?

4. **M2:** Is Ron still working as a cook?
    F1: Not anymore. He decided he's not cut out for restaurant work.
    F2: What can be concluded about Ron?

5. **F2:** Are you ready for the quiz in Dr. Davenport's class today?
    M1: A quiz? Today? Are you pulling my leg?
    F2: What does the man mean?

6. **F1:** Brian, did you watch the launch of the space shuttle on television this morning?
    M1: No, they had to put that off because of bad weather.
    F2: What does Brian mean?

7. **F1:** You're sure Jennifer was at the lecture?

   M2: Oh, she was definitely there. She really stood out in that bright red sweater of hers.

   F2: What does the man say about Jennifer?

8. **M1:** Phil just got another speeding ticket.

   F1: That serves him right.

   F2: What does the woman say about Phil?

9. **M1:** I think I'll ask George to help.

   F2: Save your breath!

   F2: What does the woman imply about George?

10. **F1:** Let me guess—you bought Jill a watch for a graduation present.

    M2: You're not even warm!

    F2: What is learned about Jill from this conversation?

11. **F1:** I heard Dora was having some trouble at work.

    M2: Yes, but as usual, she'll come out of it smelling like a rose.

    F2: What does the man say about Dora?

12. **F1:** Are you going to take a trip during spring break, Roy?

    M1: With all the studying I have to do, that's out of the question.

    F2: What does Roy tell the woman?

13. **F1:** I heard Mick is planning to go to medical school.

    M2: Yeah, I guess he's always wanted to follow in his father's footsteps.

    F2: What is learned about Mick from this conversation?

14. **M1:** I told Fred about the money I'd lost, but he didn't seem very sympathetic.

    F1: Well, if it were *his* money that had been lost, he'd be singing another tune!

    F2: What does the woman imply about Fred?

15. **M1:** I've just heard Wally's going-away party has been canceled.

    F1: Oh no! Has anyone broken the news to Wally yet?

    F2: What does the woman want to know about Wally?

16. **M1:** Deborah, do you think we can stay at your parents' cabin at the lake?

    F1: Sure, if you don't mind roughing it.

    M2: What does Deborah mean?

Exercise 4

Answer Key

1. He's not a very good dancer.
2. The suit costs a lot of money.
3. The woman has prepared too much food.
4. He's concerned about his grade.

5. He has changed his major often.

6. He lectures about history.

7. She had a long wait before she saw the dentist.

8. They have different opinions about it.

9. He and his old boss argued.

10. There's not enough snow to cause a cancellation yet.

11. He's interested in making new friends.

12. She couldn't see the concert very well.

13. Last summer was even hotter.

14. The pool can be used by students for free.

15. They're not in the city tonight.

16. He wasn't expecting a phone call.

17. He didn't solve any of the problems.

18. The scarf looks great on her.

19. Her parents have very strong accents.

20. He is an excellent skier.

Audio Script

1. **F2:** I understand Larry won another dance contest.
   M1: It's hard to believe we're from the same family, isn't it?
   M2: What can be inferred about the man?

2. **M1:** Take a look at this suit.
   F1: Nice. Are you going to buy it?
   M1: Do I look like a millionaire?
   M2: What can be inferred from this conversation?

3. **F1:** Do you think I've made enough food for the party?
   M1: I'd say you've made just the right amount—if a couple of hundred people show up!
   M2: What does the man imply?

4. **M1:** I'm exhausted. I've been in class all evening.
   F2: I didn't know you were taking any evening classes.
   M1: I'm not, actually—this was a special review session Professor Hennessy offered. It was for students who were worried about doing well on the test tomorrow.
   M2: What can be inferred about the man?

5. **M1:** Did you know Greg has changed his major?
   F2: Oh no, not again! How many times does this make?
   M2: What does the woman imply about Greg?

6. **M1:** Aren't Professor Sutton's lectures fascinating?

   F1: I can close my eyes when I'm listening to him, and I'm back in the Middle Ages.

   M1: I know what you mean!

   M2: What can be inferred from this conversation about Professor Sutton?

7. **M1:** Did you have to wait long to see the dentist yesterday?

   F1: It seemed like years!

   M2: What does the woman imply?

8. **F2:** Do the experts agree with this plan?

   M1: That depends on which expert you ask.

   M2: What does the man imply about the experts and the plan?

9. **M1:** Did you know that Louis has a new boss?

   F1: Let's hope he gets along better with this one.

   M2: What does the woman imply about Louis?

10. **F1:** Boy, this is some snowstorm. It's really coming down hard.

    M1: Sure is. I wonder if the university will cancel classes tomorrow.

    F1: Only if it keeps on snowing like this all night.

    M2: What does the woman imply?

11. **M1:** I joined the folk dancing club a couple of weeks ago.

    F2: You did? Since when are you interested in folk dancing?

    M1: Since I discovered it was a great way to meet people!

    M2: What does the man imply?

12. **M1:** Did you have a good seat for the concert?

    F1: A good seat! I practically needed a telescope just to see the stage!

    M2: What can be inferred from the woman's remark?

13. **F1:** Is it ever hot!

    M1: If you think *this* is hot, you should have been here last summer.

    M2: What does the man imply?

14. **M1:** Is the swimming pool on campus open to the public?

    F2: It is, but if you're not a student, you'll have to pay a fee to swim there.

    M2: What can be inferred from this conversation?

15. **F1:** Just look at those stars!

    M1: They certainly don't look so clear and bright from the city, do they?

    F1: No, never.

    M2: What can be inferred about the speakers?

16. **M2:** There's a phone call for you, Mike.

    M1: For me? But I almost never work on Saturdays. No one knows I'm here today.

    F2: What does Mike imply?

17. **M1:** Those calculus problems Professor McKee assigned were really tough.

    F2: Yeah, they were. I was able to solve only one of them.

    M1: Well, you still did better than I did!

    M2: What can be inferred about the man?

18. **F1:** Did you notice that bright blue scarf Fran was wearing?

    F2: Uh huh. She should wear it more often.

    M2: What can be inferred about Fran?

19. **M1:** Milly has a strong accent.

    F2: Nothing like her parents, though.

    M2: What can be inferred from this conversation about Milly?

20. **M1:** That's a tough slope to ski.

    F2: Yeah, even Robert had trouble skiing down *that* slope.

    M2: What does the woman imply about Robert?

Review Test A: Dialogues

Answer Key

1. His impression of her has changed.
2. She likes it a lot.
3. The juice is no worse than the other brands.
4. The tools have been misplaced.
5. She is not the woman's waitress.
6. Review the last point.
7. Keep a budget.
8. He doesn't like the lamp very much.
9. The man in the red car resembles Ernie.
10. He's an experienced scuba diver.
11. The man would like to use Becky's computer.
12. The ring was probably expensive.
13. He didn't realize Professor Clayburn was speaking tonight.
14. Dogs are not allowed in the dorm.
15. Bill has not finished his work.
16. The box is very heavy.

Audio Script

1. **F1:** What do you think about Wanda?

    M1: When I first met her, I didn't like her that much, but I really warmed up to her after a while.

    M2: What does the man imply about Wanda?

2. **M1:** Have you seen that old Humphrey Bogart movie *Casablanca*?
   F2: Seen it! Only about a million times!
   M2: What does the woman imply about the movie?

3. **M1:** Try a glass of this juice and see how you like it. It's a new brand.
   F1: Umm . . . I'd say it stacks up pretty well against the other kinds.
   M2: What does the woman mean?

4. **F2:** Adam, do you know the tools I lent you when you were building those bookshelves last month? I'd like to have them back.
   M1: Uh, well, I hate to tell you this . . . but I can't seem to lay my hands on them.
   M2: What does Adam imply?

5. **F1:** Excuse me . . . could I get another glass of iced tea?
   F2: Sure, I'll tell your waitress to bring you one.
   M2: What can be inferred from this conversation?

6. **F2:** Now, if there are no more questions, let's move on to the next chapter.
   M1: Excuse me, professor—could we go over that last point once more?
   M2: What does the man want to do?

7. **M1:** I'm almost out of money again this month.
   F2: Why don't you keep track of your expenses and payments? That might help you make ends meet.
   M1: Well . . . it wouldn't hurt to give it a try.
   M2: What does the woman think the man should do?

8. **M1:** I see you bought a new lamp.
   F1: Yeah, isn't it great? Where do you think I should put it, in my living room or in my bed-room?
   M1: If I were you, I'd put it in the closet.
   M2: What can be inferred from the man's comment?

9. **F1:** Look over there. Isn't that Ernie in the red car?
   M1: No, but it certainly looks like him.
   M2: What does the man mean?

10. **F2:** I didn't think John had ever been scuba diving before.
    M1: Oh, sure. John's an old hand at scuba diving.
    M2: What does the man say about John?

11. **M2:** Becky, are you going to be using your computer much longer? If so, I can go use one at the library.
    F1: I'm almost finished.
    M2: All right, I'll just wait then.
    M2: What can be inferred from this conversation?

12. **F1:** Wow, did you see that ring Laura bought?

    F2: Uh huh—must have cost her a pretty penny.

    M2: What do the speakers mean?

13. **F1:** What room is Professor Clayburn speaking in tonight?

    M1: Professor Clayburn is speaking tonight?

    M2: What does the man imply by his remark?

14. **M2:** I thought I heard barking coming from Joe's room.

    F1: Barking! Doesn't Joe know there's a rule against keeping pets in the dorm!

    M2: What can be concluded from this conversation?

15. **F2:** Bill, I thought you had so much work to do.

    M1: I'm just taking a little break.

    M2: What can be inferred from this conversation?

16. **F1:** Hey Paul, could you help me move this box upstairs?

    M1: Sure, I . . . say, what do you have in here? Your rock collection?

    M2: What can be inferred from this conversation?

Exercise 5.1

Answer Key

1. B	4. A	7. A	10. B
2. A	5. B	8. B	11. A
3. B	6. B	9. A	12. A

Audio Script

1. **M1:** The science building is so old, it ought to be torn down!

    M2: I couldn't agree with you less! It's a landmark!

2. **F1:** The wind is really bad today.

    M1: Is it ever! It took some paintings right out of my hands.

3. **M1:** I didn't think Professor Hall's lecture was very informative.

    M2: You didn't? I can't say I agree with you on that.

4. **F1:** Anthony is quite a singer.

    M2: You bet he is!

5. **M1:** I think the service at that new café is pretty good.

    F2: I wish I could say the same.

6. **M1:** Certainly Curtis won't run for student class president now!

    F2: Don't be so sure about that.

7. **M2:** It's been a long, hard day.
    F1: Hasn't it though!

8. **F2:** I think skydiving must be exciting.
    M2: You wouldn't catch *me* jumping out of an airplane!

9. **M1:** Good thing there was a fire extinguisher in the hallway.
    F1: I'll second that!

10. **F2:** There are some strange paintings in that gallery.
    F1: Strange? I wouldn't call them strange.

11. **F1:** I really like that sports car Michael bought.
    M1: Who wouldn't?

12. **F2:** We haven't heard from Harry for quite a while.
    M2: No, we certainly haven't.

Exercise 5.2

Answer Key

1. He prefers taking a final exam.
2. It's probably easier than the other chapters.
3. He thinks it's a good one.
4. She found it well-written.
5. He thinks it's a good day for bike riding, too.
6. She's not sure why Arthur dropped the class either.
7. It might work.
8. It made him angry.
9. It's crowded because students will be taking exams soon.
10. He likes the costumes Madeleine made.
11. It was unhappy.
12. She thinks the regulations are fair.

Audio Script

1. **F1:** I'd rather have a final exam than write a research paper.
    M1: Me, too. Research papers take a lot more time.
    M2: What does the man mean?

2. **M1:** This first chapter in the statistics textbook seems pretty simple.
    F2: Of course, but I'm sure the other chapters are more difficult.
    M2: How does the woman feel about the first chapter?

3. **F1:** The university should make it easier for students to register for classes.
   M1: I couldn't agree with you more!
   M2: How does the man feel about the woman's idea?

4. **M1:** Jack's story was certainly well written.
   F2: Wasn't it though! And so full of interesting details.
   M2: What was the woman's opinion of Jack's story?

5. **F1:** What a perfect day to take a bike ride!
   M1: You can say that again!
   M2: What does the man mean?

6. **M1:** I can't understand why Arthur dropped his chemistry class. He was doing so well in it.
   F2: Well, me neither, but he must have a good reason.
   M2: What does the woman mean?

7. **M1:** Tom's plan is so impractical, it will never work.
   F1: That's not necessarily so.
   M2: What does the woman say about Tom's plan?

8. **M1:** Did you read this editorial in the morning paper?
   F2: I sure did, and did it ever make me angry!
   M1: I felt the same way when I first read it, but you know, the more I thought about it, the more I agreed with it.
   M2: What was the man's *initial* reaction to the editorial?

9. **M1:** The library sure is crowded this evening.
   F1: Is it ever! You can tell it's getting near final exam week.
   M2: What does the woman say about the library?

10. **F2:** Madeleine designed the costumes for the play. They're wonderful, don't you think?
    M1: Absolutely. Who wouldn't?
    M2: What does the man mean?

11. **F1:** That was an exciting movie, and what a happy ending.
    M1: Happy! You call that *happy*?
    M2: How does the man feel about the ending of the movie?

12. **M1:** Pamela thinks these new regulations are unfair, but I don't.
    F1: Oh, neither do I.
    M2: What does the woman mean?

Exercise 6.1

Answer Key

1. A	**5.** B	**9.** B	**13.** A
2. A	**6.** A	**10.** A	**14.** B
3. B	**7.** A	**11.** A	**15.** B
4. B	**8.** B	**12.** B	**16.** B

Audio Script

1. **F1:** May I help you?
   M1: Thanks, but I'm just looking around.

2. **M2:** Can you come to the recital this evening?
   F2: I'm supposed to be working on my research this evening, but you know, I think a break would be nice.

3. **M1:** That author we both like is going to be signing books at Appleton's Bookstore this afternoon.
   F1: I'm not busy this afternoon. Why don't we go?

4. **F2:** Mark, would you mind taking care of my tropical fish next week? I'm going to be out of town.
   M2: Oh, no, I wouldn't mind at all.

5. **M1:** I need to get more exercise.
   F2: You could always try bicycling. That's great exercise.

6. **F1:** Can I see the photographs you took on the trip?
   M2: If you want to, why not?

7. **M1:** I can't seem to get my car started.
   M2: You know what I'*d* do, Ed?

8. **M1:** These math problems are hard.
   F2: Want me to give you a few hints?

9. **M2:** Cynthia, if you have a class, I could take your brother to the airport for you.
   F1: Could you? That would be great.

10. **M1:** Should I turn on the television?
    F2: Please don't.

11. **F2:** You could save a lot of time at the supermarket by making up a list before you go.
    M1: It's worth a try, I guess.

12. **M1:** Bob, get me a cup of coffee, will you?
    M2: Who do you think I am, your waiter?

13. **F1:** I'm going to go out and get something to eat. Want to come?

    M1: I've got a better idea. Let's have a pizza delivered.

14. **F2:** My arm still hurts.

    M2: Well, Jacquelyn, I'd get it X-rayed if I were you.

15. **F2:** You know, Matt, if you want your houseplants to grow, you should move them over by the window where they get more light.

    M2: Now why didn't I ever think of that?

16. **F1:** Have another sandwich, James.

    M1: Thanks—don't mind if I do.

Exercise 6.2

Answer Key

1. He doesn't want the woman to smoke.
2. The man could wear it tonight.
3. She could plan the trip.
4. He doesn't want more coffee.
5. She'll open the window herself.
6. Have some soup for lunch.
7. The kitchen also needs cleaning.
8. Help her find her way to the registrar's office.
9. Stop studying for a little while.
10. Buy a new toaster.
11. She can read his magazine if she wants.
12. Get a new computer.
13. He doesn't plan to study tonight.
14. He doesn't want to respond to the letters.
15. She can't come to lunch today.

Audio Script

1. **F1:** Do you mind if I smoke?

   M1: As a matter of fact, I *do*.

   M2: What does the man mean?

2. **M1:** I don't know what to wear this evening. My blue suit hasn't come back from the cleaners yet.

   F2: Well, there's always your gray one. That looks nice on you.

   M2: What does the woman say about the gray suit?

3. **F1:** We need someone to plan the class trip.
   M1: How about Cathy?
   M2: What does the man say about Cathy?

4. **F2:** Shall I make some more coffee?
   M1: Not on my account.
   M2: What does the man mean?

5. **M1:** Should I open the window? It's getting a little warm in here.
   F1: Don't bother, I'll do it.
   M2: What does the woman mean?

6. **M1:** I don't know what to order for lunch. I'm tired of the sandwiches in the cafeteria.
   F2: What about some vegetable soup?
   M1: You know, that doesn't sound too bad.
   M2: What will the man probably do?

7. **M1:** I'm going to clean my living room this afternoon.
   F2: Shouldn't you clean your kitchen, too?
   M2: What does the woman imply?

8. **M1:** What office are you looking for?
   F1: The registrar's office. I need some information about signing up for classes next semester.
   M1: That's across campus from here. Would you like me to show you on this map?
   M2: What does the man offer to do for the woman?

9. **M1:** Well, that's it for our statistics homework. We should work on our math problems next.
   F1: What about taking a little break first?
   M2: What does the woman suggest they do?

10. **F2:** Do you think this toaster can be repaired?
    M1: If I were in your shoes, Lisa, I think I'd just buy another one.
    M2: What does the man suggest that Lisa do?

11. **F2:** Would you mind if I read your magazine? That looks like an interesting article.
    M1: No, go right ahead. I'm finished with it.
    M2: What does the man tell the woman?

12. **M1:** You know, I think I'm going to get a new computer desk. This one is just too small for me to work at.
    F2: What about buying a new computer instead? Yours is practically an antique!
    M2: What does the woman think the man should do?

13. **F1:** Christopher, want to come to the library with Tim and me? We're going to study for our biology test tomorrow.
    M1: I think I'll pass on that. I spent the whole weekend going over my biology notes, and tonight I'm just going to relax.
    M2: What does Christopher tell the woman?

14. **F2:** Someone should answer these letters.
     M1: Well, don't look at me!
     M2: What does the man mean?

15. **M1:** I'm having some friends over for lunch today. Think you can make it?
     F1: Can I take a rain check?
     M2: What does the woman mean?

Exercise 7

Answer Key

1. She doesn't mind eating chicken.
2. She hadn't found a new apartment yet.
3. Who told the man to see the dean.
4. He wants to take part in the election.
5. She hadn't completed all the research.
6. He doesn't really like horseback riding.
7. When her travel agent called.
8. He didn't want a job.
9. How long their hike was.
10. He thinks the clothes at that store are expensive.
11. Where the meeting will be held.
12. Joy would study overseas this year.
13. If the man enjoyed the party.
14. Most of the problems were done correctly.
15. Why she went to the grocery store.
16. It had needed batteries.
17. How long he has been traveling.
18. It hadn't been released yet.

Audio Script

1. **M2:** Ginny may join us for dinner tomorrow night. Is that all right?
    F1: Sure, but if she does, I guess I'd better serve fish. She doesn't care for chicken.
    M2: Actually, I'm sure she *does*.
    F2: What does the man say about Ginny?

2. **F2:** Mona is moving into a new apartment on Sunday.
    M1: So she finally found a place, did she?
    F2: What had the man assumed about Mona?

3. **M1:** I was told to go to the dean's office.
   F1: By whom?
   F2: What does the woman want to know?

4. **F1:** I told everyone that of course you weren't interested in running for class president.
   M1: But as a matter of fact, I *am*.
   F2: What does the man mean?

5. **F2:** Carol's word-processing the final draft of her paper right now.
   M2: Oh, so she finally finished the research for it?
   F2: What had the man assumed about Carol?

6. **M2:** Bert says he loves to ride horses.
   F1: Sure, but you don't actually see him on horseback very often, do you?
   F2: What does the woman imply about Bert?

7. **F1:** Anyone call while I was out?
   M1: Yeah, your travel agent called. She said she'd made your flight reservation.
   F1: I see. How long ago was this?
   F2: What does the woman want to know?

8. **M2:** Did you know Cliff is working part-time in the cafeteria now?
   F1: Oh, he finally decided to get a job, then?
   F2: What had the woman assumed about Cliff?

9. **M1:** We spent the whole day hiking.
   F1: Really? How far did you go?
   F2: What does the woman want to know?

10. **M1:** I need some new clothes.
    F1: There are some nice clothes in that store on Collins Street, and it seems to me the prices there are pretty reasonable.
    M1: Reasonable! I wouldn't call them reasonable.
    F2: What does the man mean?

11. **M1:** There's going to be a meeting to discuss the proposed recreation center.
    F1: Really? Where?
    F2: What does the woman ask the man?

12. **M2:** Joy is going to study overseas in a special program next year.
    F1: That's not until next year?
    F2: What had the woman assumed?

13. **M1:** I went to a party at Ben's house this weekend.
    F1: Did you have a good time?
    F2: What does the woman ask the man?

14. **F1:** Ted didn't do a good job on these problems. He'll have to do them all over.
    M2: Well, a few of them, anyway.
    F2: What does the man mean?

15. **F1:** I stopped at the grocery store on the way home from class.
    M2: Yeah? How come?
    F2: What does the man ask the woman?

16. **M2:** You know, I put new batteries in the flashlight, but it still doesn't work.
    F1: No kidding? I was sure it would.
    M2: What had the woman assumed about the flashlight?

17. **M1:** My friend Steve is traveling around in the Pacific Northwest.
    F1: Since when?
    F2: What does the woman want to know about Steve?

18. **M1:** Beverly, have you seen that new movie starring Calvin Pierce?
    F1: Oh, that's already out?
    F2: What had Beverly originally assumed about the movie?

Exercise 8

Answer Key

1. Road conditions.
2. Clean up Beth's apartment.
3. The car isn't big enough for four people.
4. A bridge.
5. Go on a camping trip.
6. Get different lenses for his glasses.
7. Painting.
8. Watch television.
9. It was ruined in the rain.
10. A computer.
11. Look for a job with a big company.
12. He doesn't have a stamp.
13. Order a salad.
14. To a bank.
15. The chair broke as he was standing on it.

Audio Script

1. **F2:** I can't believe how icy the highway is tonight.
   F1: Yeah, I've never seen it so bad. Maybe we should just stay at a motel and see if it's any better in the morning.
   M2: What are they talking about?

2. (*Ring . . . ring*)
   F2: Hello.
   F1: Great party you threw last night, Beth.

	F2:	Yeah, but you should see my apartment this morning. What a mess! I feel like moving somewhere else!
	F1:	Don't worry. I'll come over this afternoon and help you out.
	M2:	What are they probably going to do this afternoon?
3.	**F1:**	Joe and Nancy and I were hoping to get a ride to the party with you.
	M1:	With me? But I drive a little two-seater.
	M2:	What is the problem?
4.	**M2:**	You mean it's *still* closed?
	M1:	Yes, sir, the repairs won't be done for another two weeks. You'll have to take Highway 17 to Springdale and cross the river on the one down there.
	M2:	What are they probably talking about?
5.	**M2:**	Okay, so tomorrow, I'll bring the portable stove and the food.
	M1:	And I'll bring the tent and we'll each bring a sleeping bag.
	M2:	Hey, this is going to be fun!
	M2:	What are the speakers probably planning to do tomorrow?
6.	**F1:**	I like your new glasses, Brian.
	M1:	I like these new frames, too, but my vision is blurry and I've been having headaches. I've got to go back to Dr. Lamb and get some new lenses prescribed.
	M2:	What does Brian intend to do?
7.	**F2:**	Do you think I'll need to put on two coats of this latex?
	M1:	Will you be using brushes or a roller?
	M2:	What are these people discussing?
8.	**F1:**	Want to watch that documentary about polar bears in Canada now?
	M1:	Well, I am a little tired, but okay, sure—what channel?
	M2:	What is the man going to do next?
9.	**M1:**	Uh, Denise, do you remember that art book I borrowed from you last month?
	F2:	Oh, right. Do you have it for me? I'm going to need it back soon.
	M1:	Ummm, well, actually, I'm going to have to replace it. See, Tuesday I was looking at it out in the yard, and forgot to bring it in with me—and you remember that rain we had Tuesday night?
	M2:	What problem did the man have with the book?
10.	**M2:**	Take a look at this model. It's incredibly fast, and it has an extended keyboard.
	F1:	Does it have much memory?
	M2:	What are the speakers probably discussing?
11.	**F2:**	Shirley, are you going to go right on to business school when you finish your undergraduate program?
	F1:	Actually, I hope to get some practical experience with a big international corporation first.
	F2:	That's a good idea, I think.
	M2:	What will Shirley probably do right after she finishes her undergraduate program?

12. **F2:** Dave, Phyllis is going to be upset with you if you don't send her a postcard while we're here on vacation
    M1: Yeah, well, I'd like to send her one, but I've been by the post office twice to buy stamps and for some reason it hasn't been open.
    M2: What is Dave's problem?

13. **F1:** I'm starving. Want to go have lunch?
    M1: Sure, let's go to that soup and salad restaurant, okay? I think their soups taste just like homemade.
    F1: All right, we can go there, but I think their soups are always much too salty.
    M2: What will the woman probably do?

14. **F1:** Gilbert, are you ready for your trip tomorrow?
    M1: Well, almost. I still need to get some travelers' cheques.
    M2: Where does Gilbert probably plan to go today?

15. **F2:** What happened to this old chair?
    M1: Well, I was using it to stand on to change the overhead light, and . . .
    F2: And it wouldn't support your weight? I see.
    M2: What was the man's problem?

Exercise 9

Answer Key

1. B	5. A	9. A	13. B
2. B	6. B	10. A	14. B
3. B	7. B	11. B	15. B
4. A	8. A	12. A	16. A

Audio Script

1. **F1:** Doug and Rose are such good friends.
    M1: Well—they *used* to be.
    M2: What does the man say?

2. **M1:** I'm going to re-wire my house myself.
    F2: If I were you, Roger, I think I'd have a professional do it.
    M2: What does the woman tell Roger?

3. **F1:** I thought this was a classical music station.
    M1: It used to be, but now it's a twenty-four hour news station.
    M2: What does the man say about the radio station?

4. **F1:** Lynn, who did you get to change your oil?
    F2: Now why would I need anyone to do *that* for me?
    M2: What can be inferred from Lynn's remark?

5. **F1:** I'm having a hard time getting used to this early morning class.
   M1: Yeah, me too.
   M2: What does the man mean?

6. **M2:** Peggy, do you ever go skating anymore?
   F2: Sometimes, but not as much as I used to.
   M2: What does Peggy mean?

7. **F1:** You got some egg on your tie, Kenny.
   M1: I know. I'll have to get it cleaned.
   M2: What does Kenny mean?

8. **F2:** There's something different about your apartment, isn't there?
   M1: That poster over my desk used to be over the sofa.
   M2: What does the man mean?

9. **M2:** Will your boss let you take a vacation in August?
   F1: If he doesn't, I'll just look for another job when I get back.
   M2: What does the woman mean?

10. **F2:** Greg, that was an interesting point you made in class.
    M1: Thanks. But when the teacher made me explain what I meant, I didn't know exactly what to say to her.
    M2: What did Greg's teacher do?

11. **F1:** Carter just doesn't look the same these days.
    F2: I know. I'm not used to seeing him without glasses either.
    M2: What do the speakers say about Carter?

12. **F2:** Nick, how do you like this hot, humid weather?
    M1: Well, growing up in New Orleans, I'm pretty much used to it.
    M2: What does Nick tell the woman?

13. **F1:** You look nice today, Sally.
    F2: Thanks—our club is having our photo taken today for the yearbook.
    M2: What does Sally mean?

14. **F1:** You finally bought a microwave oven, I see.
    M1: Uh huh, but I haven't gotten used to cooking with it yet.
    F1: Well, once you do, you'll use it all the time.
    M2: What does the woman say about the microwave oven?

15. **M1:** Jan, look behind you—there's a deer.
    F2: Oh, isn't it beautiful. Do you think it will let us get a little closer to it?
    M2: What does Jan ask the man?

16. **M1:** Isn't the water in the lake too cold to swim in?
    F2: It felt that way at first, but in a few minutes, I got used to it.
    M2: What does the woman tell the man?

Review Test B: Dialogues

Answer Key

1. Books.
2. Discussing the problem with his neighbor.
3. She doesn't need Professor Osborne's permission to take it.
4. The tools have been misplaced.
5. He doesn't like the woman's suggestion very much.
6. Why he is in a hurry.
7. The man ought to wear his hat.
8. He thinks the team was unprepared, too.
9. His shoes hurt his feet.
10. The woman's field of study.
11. She was about to suggest the same thing.
12. He hasn't always been so sociable.
13. The woman may see his painting.
14. Tomorrow probably won't be such a nice day.
15. Why the woman went to see Dr. Norton.
16. She hadn't completed the required courses.

Audio Script

1. **M1:** So, what makes these so valuable?
    F2: Well, they're first editions, that adds value. And they're in mint condition.
    M1: And since they have the original dust jackets, I suppose that makes them worth more too, huh?
    M2: What are they discussing?

2. **M1:** I'm tired. My neighbor kept me up until two, playing his stereo at the highest volume. I'm thinking about looking for a new apartment.
    F1: Before you do, why don't you have a chat with your neighbor? Maybe he'd be willing to turn down his stereo at night.
    F2: What does the woman suggest?

3. **M1:** Sonya, are you planning to sign up for Professor Osborne's seminar next semester?
    F1: I think so, but I've got to get his permission first.
    M1: Actually, I don't think you do.
    F2: What does the man tell Sonya about the seminar?

4. **F1:** Adam, do you remember the tools I lent you when you were building those book-shelves? I'd like to have them back.
    M2: Uh, well, I hate to tell you this, but I can't seem to lay my hands on them.
    F2: What does Adam imply?

5. **M1:** My sister is looking for a roommate. Do you know anyone who might want to move in with her?

   F1: How about Grace? She'll need a place at the end of the month.

   M1: Hmmmm . . . can't you think of anyone else?

   M2: What does the man imply?

6. **M1:** We'd better leave right now.

   F2: What's the rush, Mark?

   M2: What does the woman ask Mark?

7. **M1:** It's freezing out here! I'm going to put on my scarf and gloves.

   F2: Shouldn't you put on a hat, too?

   M2: What does the woman mean?

8. **M1:** I didn't think the team was very well prepared for that game.

   M2: To tell you the truth, neither did I.

   F2: What does the second man mean?

9. **F2:** Why are you walking that way, Richard? Did you hurt yourself when you went skiing?

   M1: No, no—it's these shoes; they're not broken in yet.

   M2: What problem is Richard having?

10. **M1:** I didn't realize you were an art history major.

    F2: I'm not. I'm taking a class in art history, but I'm studying to be a commercial artist.

    M2: What are these people discussing?

11. **M2:** We should have a dinner party.

    F1: You took the words right out of my mouth.

    M2: What does the woman mean?

12. **F2:** Victor sure is outgoing.

    M1: Isn't he! It's hard to believe he used to be shy.

    M2: What do the speakers imply about Victor?

13. **F1:** Can I look at your painting for a second?

    M1: Be my guest.

    M2: What does the man mean?

14. **M1:** Great weather we're having, huh?

    F1: Yeah, but don't get too used to it. I heard on the radio that there's a big change in store tomorrow.

    M2: What does the woman tell the man?

15. **F1:** I stopped by Doctor Norton's office at the medical center.

    F2: Really? What for?

    M2: What does the woman want to know?

16. **F1:** Did you know Angela had finished all her required courses? She'll be graduating in May.

    M1: Oh, so she doesn't have to repeat that chemistry course after all.

    M2: What had the man assumed about Angela?

Listening Part B: Longer Talks

Exercise 10

Answer Key

1. Ways to improve the man's presentation.
2. To review a reading assignment. / To contrast two forms of taxation.
3. Procedures for checking out reserve materials.
4. The disadvantages of being in the program./ The procedures for arranging a tryout.
5. Tina's volunteer position.
6. Reasons why scientists don't believe ESP is valid.
7. The historical record contained in shipwrecks.
8. Self-regulation of the advertising industry.
9. To get some career advice.
10. Directions to another office.

Audio Script

    F2: Listen to a conversation between a teacher and a student.

    M1: Professor Mueller, I've almost finished preparing my presentation for your class, but I'm not really satisfied with it. Could you give me some advice?

    F2: I'll be happy to. What topic did you choose?

    M1: It's about methods of predicting earthquakes, but so far, it's just a lot of facts and figures. How can I make it more interesting?

    F2: Maybe you could use some computer graphics to help the class make sense of your statistics.

1. What will the main topic of this conversation probably be?

F2: Listen to part of a discussion in an economics class. The class has been studying taxation.

M2: In last Friday's class, I asked you to read the first part of Chapter 22, about taxation. The text says there are two main types of taxation. Anyone remember what they are? Yes, Troy?

M1: I think the book said they were direct and indirect—right?

M2: Right, Troy. And can anyone define direct taxation? Cheryl?

F1: That's when the person or firm who is taxed pays the government directly. Like income tax.

M2: You got it. And so indirect taxation...

F1: If I understand the book, it's when the person or firm who is taxed passes the tax on to someone else. A good is imported into a country, the government taxes the company that owns it, and then that company charges customers—that's indirect taxation—right?

M2: Yes, exactly. Can anyone think of another example? Troy?

M1: Well, last year, the city raised property taxes, and my landlady raised my rent to help pay the higher taxes. Is that an example?

M2: It certainly is. Cheryl, you have a question?

F1: Yes, Professor, I was just wondering—what about sales taxes? Are they indirect or direct?

M2: Ummm, good question. I'll let you all think about that for a minute, and then you tell me. . . .

2. What are the main purposes of this discussion?

F2: Listen to the following conversation in a university library.

F1: I'm in Professor Quinn's political science class. She told us that she'd put some articles on reserve for her class.

F2: Yes, those would be at the reserve desk.

F1: Do I need a library card to look at those articles?

F2: No, just a student ID card. If you've never checked out any reserve materials, I can tell you what you need to do.

3. What will the main subject of this conversation probably be?

F2: Listen to part of a lecture about a dance program.

F1: Since all of you have expressed interest in joining the university dance program, I probably don't have to say much about the physical and psychological rewards of being in a dance program such as this one. Instead, I want to concentrate on some of the drawbacks—the early mornings and late nights, the aches and pains and the physical exhaustion and all the other sacrifices you'll be called on to make if you are chosen for the program. And if, despite what you hear, you still want to try out for the program, I'll let you know how to set up your preliminary dance audition.

4. What will the rest of this talk mainly be about?

F2: Listen to a conversation between two students.

M1: Well, I had a pretty relaxing vacation. How about you, Tina?

F1: I wouldn't exactly call it relaxing, but it certainly was interesting.

M1: I remember you said you were either going to Europe or you were going to work at your parents' company.

F1: I changed my mind and didn't do either. My anthropology professor talked me into volunteering for an archaeological project in New Mexico.

5. What will the two speakers probably discuss?

F2: Listen to part of a discussion in a psychology class.

F1: Excuse me, Professor Norton, I'm a little confused...

M1: Why is that, Deborah?

F1: Well, when you were talking about ESP, you said that most scientists today don't believe it exists.

M1: That's right. First, does everyone in class know what ESP is?

M2: Sure—ESP means extra-sensory perception. Mind-reading, and that kind of thing.

M1: Good definition. It's sometimes called para-psychology.

F1: Well, the reason I'm confused is that I read an article about ESP studies at some university. It said that the researchers concluded that a number of people did have ESP abilities.

M1: You're probably thinking of the experiments at Duke University. A Professor named J. P. Rhine established a parapsychology lab there, about fifty years ago, and he developed experiments that seemed to show that some people had remarkable ESP talents.

F1: Yes, that's it—I remember it was at Duke University.

M2: So Professor, what happened to change everyone's minds about ESP?

M1: Well, since then, a lot of researchers have decided that Rhine's evidence was questionable. Today, when experiments are more carefully controlled, similar performances are rare. And in science, the trend should be the opposite.

M2: What do you mean, Professor?

M1: Well, if the phenomenon you're investigating is real, and the experiments are improved, then the results you get should be more certain, not less certain.

F1: So, you don't think ESP is possible?

M1: Well, let's just say that I don't think there's any experimental proof for it.

6. What are the speakers mainly discussing?

F2: Listen to part of a lecture in an American history class.

M2: Good afternoon. I'm Robert Wolfe, president of the State Historical Society. Professor Lewis has asked me to give a guest lecture. I'm going to give you a short presentation on some famous shipwrecks, especially ones that took place in the waters off New England, and I'm going to spend most of my time explaining how a study of shipwrecks can contribute to an understanding of history.

7. What is this lecture primarily going to concern?

F2: Listen to part of a lecture given in an advertising class.

M2: Good morning, students. In our last class, we were talking about regulation in the advertising industry. In fact, as you may remember, I said advertising was one of the most heavily regulated industries in the United States, and I gave as an example the law that prohibits advertising tobacco products on television. Now, in today's class, I want to tell you about self-regulation in advertising, which the industry has adopted as a way to stop abuses before they can occur. As we'll see, these self-imposed codes of ethics are intended to control not only bad taste but also misrepresentation and deception—although, they don't always work. Any questions before we get started?

8. What will the rest of the lecture probably concern?

F2: Listen to a conversation that takes place at a hospital.

F1: Good afternoon, Dr. Marshall. I know you must be very busy, so I appreciate your taking some time to talk to me.

M2: That's all right. What can I do for you?

F1: Well, I'm interested in a career in hospital administration. My academic advisor suggested I speak to you. I was hoping you could give me some information about the field.

M2: I'd be glad to. Is there something particular you wanted to know?

F1: Well, first I was wondering what type of educational background a hospital administrator needs. Is a degree in medicine required?

M2: No, not necessarily. Some hospital administrators are medical doctors, but many of us aren't. My own doctoral degree is in public administration.

9. Why does the woman want to talk to Dr. Marshall?

F2: Listen to part of a conversation that takes place in a university office.

M1: Hi, how can I help you?

F1: I'm looking for an application form for the graduate school—can I pick one up here?

M1: No, this is the Financial Aid Office. Graduate Admissions is across campus from here. Do you know where Nicholson Hall is? It's in the office building next to that.

F1: Ummm, I'm not sure—I'm not very familiar with this campus.

10. What will the rest of the conversation probably deal with?

Exercise 11

Answer Key

1. He stayed up most of the night.
2. It was disappointing.
3. Professors / Graduate students.
4. Test-taking skills.
5. In Staunton Hall.
6. Get some sleep.
7. In the 1950s.
8. They burn up in the atmosphere.
9. About eight thousand.
10. They are too small.
11. A piece of metal the size of an aspirin. / A lost tool.
12. Its high speed.
13. (B)
14. It could serve as a protective device for manned spacecraft./ It could be mounted on un-manned spacecraft to find and trap pieces of debris.
15. It has not been built yet.
16. (C)
17. To see the swallows arrive. / To help a colleague.
18. They are a type of bird.
19. In March.
20. About 7,000 miles.
21. By an earthquake.
22. They eliminate insect pests./ They help bring money into the community.
23. Only during the first week of the semester.
24. A classroom.
25. In the Student Center Building.
26. Because the Earth did not seem to move. / Because the objects in the sky seemed to revolve around the Earth.
27. Crystal.
28. (B)
29. (D)
30. In the sixteenth century.
31. Copernican model.
32. It is no longer considered accurate.
33. They were very far away.

Audio Script

M1: Listen to a conversation between two students.

F2: You look exhausted this morning, Steve.

M1: I *am* pretty tired. I stayed up nearly all night getting ready for my chemistry mid-term exam this morning.

F2: Have you gotten the results of the test yet?

M1: Yes, and unfortunately, my grade could have been much better. But I'm not all that surprised. No matter how much time I spend studying, I never seem to do well on tests.

F2: You know, Steve, if I were you, I'd consider taking some of the seminars offered by the Study Skills Center.

M1: The Study Skills Center? Never heard of it.

F2: Well, it's run by a group of graduate students and professors who help undergraduate students improve their study techniques.

M1: What kind of seminars does the Center offer that could help me?

F2: Well, they have one on test-taking skills.

M1: That definitely sounds like something I need.

F2: There's also a seminar that teaches you to manage your time efficiently. You should find *that* useful, I should think.

M1: Yeah, maybe. So, where is the Center?

F2: They hold most of their seminars in the library, but the main office is in Staunton Hall, right across the quadrangle from the Physics Tower.

M1: You know, I think I'll go over there right now and talk to someone.

F2: Why don't you wait until tomorrow? Right now, you should go back to your dorm and catch up on your sleep.

1. Why is Steve tired?
2. How did Steve feel about the grade he received?
3. Who teaches the seminars at the Study Skills Center?
4. What seminar will Steve probably take?
5. Where is the main office of the Study Skills Center?
6. What does the woman think Steve should do next?

M2: Listen to part of a talk given in a space science class.

F2: The skies above Earth are turning into a junkyard. Ever since the Soviet Union launched *Sputnik*, the first satellite, way back in 1957, virtually every launch has contributed to the amount of debris in Earth orbit. Luckily, most of this junk burns up after it re-enters the Earth's atmosphere, but some will be up there in orbit for years to come. Today, there are about 8,000 bodies in orbit being monitored from Earth. Out of all those, only around 3 to 400 are active and useful. There are also probably half a million pieces of debris too tiny to be monitored.

Some orbital debris is as big as a bus, but most is in the form of tiny flecks of paint or pieces of metal. The debris includes food wrappers, an astronaut's glove, the lens cap from a camera, broken tools, and bags of unwashed uniforms. The largest pieces—mostly empty booster rockets—are not necessarily the most dangerous because they can be detected and spacecraft can avoid them. And the smallest particles generally cause only surface damage. However, a collision with a particle an eighth of an inch in diameter—say about the size of an aspirin—could puncture the hull of a spacecraft or space station and cause de-pressurization. Imagine what might happen if a spacecraft struck a screwdriver or a wrench that some astronaut had dropped during a space walk! These small objects are so dangerous, of course, because of their tremendous speed.

So what can be done about this problem? Well, two engineers recently proposed a novel solution to the problem of orbital junk: a collector that consists of an array of water-spraying cones lined with plastic fibers to collect the debris. The debris is then stored in a canister located behind the cones. I brought a model of this collector along with me so you can see what it looks like. Although this invention is still in its conceptual stage, two possible uses have been proposed. It could be launched with a free-flying unmanned satellite to actively seek out debris or it could be launched into orbit with a manned spacecraft to serve as a defensive shield.

7. When did orbital debris first appear?
8. What happens to most pieces of orbital debris?
9. How many orbital bodies are being monitored today?
10. Why is it impossible to monitor most pieces of orbital debris?
11. Which of the following types of orbital debris are probably most dangerous to astronauts on a spacecraft?
12. What makes orbital debris such a danger to spacecraft?
13. Assume that this is a representation of a satellite equipped with a collector. Where would the space debris be stored?
14. In which ways could the collector be used to solve the problem of orbital debris?
15. What can be inferred about the collector described in this portion of the talk?

M2: Listen to a discussion that takes place before a biology class.

F1: Hello, Rebecca, hello John. Did you have a good spring break?

M1: Hi Professor—actually, I just stayed in town and worked. I didn't do anything too exciting.

F2: And I went home to see my parents. How about you, Professor—what did you do over the break?

F1: Well, one of my colleagues, Professor Nugent from the history department, is doing research on California mission churches, so I went to California to help by taking some photographs. Also, we were able to arrange our trip so that we were in the town of San Juan Capistrano when the swallows returned. That's something I always wanted to see. As you know, I'm interested in migration patterns, and this is one of the more remarkable migrations in all the animal kingdom.

M1: Where is San Juan Capistrano, Professor?

F1: It's on the Pacific Coast, between Los Angeles and San Diego.

F2: I've head about those swallows before—they always return on the same date, don't they?

F1: That's right—on March 19. And they always fly away on the same day, October 23rd. In the meantime, they migrate over 7,000 miles to get to their winter homes.

M1: Seven thousand miles—imagine! And always arriving on the same day.

F1: Yes, almost always. One year, a long time ago, they were delayed for several days by a storm at sea.

F2: So there's a mission church in San Juan Capistrano?

F1: Well, there's the ruins of one. The town grew up around a church that the Spanish built in the 1770s. But it was mostly destroyed by an earthquake in the early 1800s. Today, there are just a few walls and part of the tower of the old church still standing. In fact, the swallows like to build their nests in the ruins.

F2: So were there a lot of tourists there to see the swallows return?

F1: Oh yes, thousands of them. There's quite a celebration. The townspeople even have a parade to welcome the swallows back.

M1: Wow. They must really like those swallows!

F1: Sure—not only do the swallows bring lots of tourist money to town, but they also eat insects—including mosquitoes!

16. Where is the town of San Juan Capistrano located?
17. What were the professor's main reasons for going to San Juan Capistrano?
18. What can be inferred about the swallows?
19. When do the swallows return to San Juan Capistrano?
20. How far do the swallows migrate?
21. According to the professor, how was the mission church in San Juan Capistrano damaged?
22. According to the professor, why are the swallows popular with the people of San Juan Capistrano?

M2: Listen to a conversation that takes place on a college campus.

M1: I'm here for the campus tour.

F2: I'm sorry, we only offer guided tours during the first week of the semester.

M1: Oh really? That's too bad. I was really hoping to get a good orientation. Last week, I spent nearly an hour trying to find a classroom in the Fine Arts Building.

F2: You know what you *can* do—you can take the self-guided tour. This pamphlet tells you exactly what to do, where to go, and what to look for, and it has a complete map of the campus.

M1: Sounds easy enough—where do I start?

F2: The first stop is right here, in the Student Center Building. Then you go next door to the Science Building—there's a great planetarium there, by the way—and from there you go to the University Recreation Center. After that, just follow the directions in the pamphlet, and you can't go wrong.

23. When is the guided tour of the campus given?
24. What did the man have trouble locating the week before?
25. Where does the self-guided tour start?

M2: Listen to part of a lecture in an astronomy class.

F2: The ancient Greeks developed a model of the universe called the geocentric model— *geo*, of course, is Greek for "Earth." Why, you might ask, did they think the Earth was the center of the universe? Well, if you think about it, it was a perfectly logical conclusion. They were on the Earth, and the Earth didn't seem to be moving. And then, of course, they looked up at the sky, and all the bodies they saw seemed to be revolving around them. So you see, it was a sensible theory for them.

By the second century, the Greek astronomer Ptolemy had refined the model to the point that he could predict—with remarkable accuracy, I might add—the future position of the seven known planets. Today, we still call the geocentric model the Ptolemaic model. The Ptolemaic model pictured an elegant clockwork universe in which objects in the sky were attached to hollow crystal spheres. The Earth was of course in the center. The Moon was attached to the closest sphere, followed by Mercury and Venus. Then came the Sun, followed by Mars and the rest of the outer planets. The outermost sphere contained the stars.

Then, after Ptolemy's death, interest in astronomy almost disappeared. The Ptolemaic model was accepted for the next 1,400 years, and eventually became part of the medieval system of religious belief.

By the sixteenth century, Nicholas Copernicus helped renew interest in astronomy with his hypothesis that the Earth turned on its axis and revolved around the Sun. This was the heliocentric model. *Helios* is Greek for "Sun." This model is also called the Copernican model. In this model, the Sun is the center of the universe, and all the planets circle it, traveling in the same direction—first Mercury, then Venus, then Earth, the third planet. The Moon, of course, circles the Earth. Farther out from the Sun are the orbits of Mars and the other planets, and somewhere beyond them, the stars. Copernicus regarded the stars as faraway points of light of an unknown nature. It was impossible for him to know that they were much like our Sun, only vastly farther away. It made sense to consider the Sun as the center of the universe rather than just one star out of billions in our galaxy, because no one knew that there were billions of other suns out there.

26. According to the lecturer, why did the ancient Greeks think that the Earth was the center of the universe?

27. What did the ancient Greeks believe the spheres circling the Earth were made of?

28. This is a simple representation of the geocentric model. Which letter represents the Earth's moon?

29. This is a simple representation of the heliocentric model. Which letter represents the Earth's moon?

30. When was the heliocentric model proposed?

31. Which of these phrases is a synonym for *heliocentric model*?

32. What does the lecturer imply about the heliocentric model?

33. Which of the following did Copernicus believe about the stars?

Exercise 12

Answer Key

1. (C) (D) (A) (B)
2. (B) (A) (C)
3. (B) (C) (A)
4. (A) (D) (C) (B)
5. (C) (A) (B)

6. (D) (A) (B) (C)
7. (C) (B) (A)
8. (A) (B) (C)
9. (D) (C) (A) (B)
10. (B) (C) (A)

Audio Script

F2: You will hear part of a lecture in a chemistry class. The class has been focusing on hydrocarbon compounds.

F1: We've been considering various useful hydrocarbon compounds, and today, we're going to look at one of the most useful of all of these. That's right, I'm talking about coal. There probably wouldn't have been an Industrial Revolution in the eighteenth century without coal. Even today, life would be very different if we didn't have coal.

So, where does coal come from? Well, imagine what the Earth was like say, 300 million years ago—during the Carboniferous period. Much of the land was covered with luxuriant vegetation, especially ferns—ferns big as trees. Eventually, these plants died and were submerged in the waters of swamps, where they gradually decomposed. And we've seen what happens when plants decompose—the vegetable matter loses oxygen and hydrogen atoms, leaving a deposit with a high percentage of carbon. In this way, peat bogs were formed. Then, as time went on, layers of sand and mud settled from the water over the peat bogs. These deposits grew thicker and thicker, and the pressure increased, and the deposits were compressed and hardened. And so you have—coal!

All grades of coal have uses. Lignite, the lowest grade of coal, is often burned in furnaces for heat. Most bituminous coal, which has a higher carbon content, is used by utility companies to produce electricity. Anthracite, which has the highest carbon content, is often distilled to produce coke. Coke is almost pure carbon, and is used in the manufacture of steel. And coal tar, one of the by-products of producing coke, is used to make many different types of plastic.

1. The lecturer discusses the steps involved in the creation of coal. Summarize this process by putting the events in the proper order.
2. Match the form of coal with the type of industry which primarily uses it.

F2: Listen to part of a discussion in an accounting seminar. The seminar is talking about some of the basic principles of accounting.

M2: Hello, everyone. As you can see from our course syllabus, our topic today is something called "GAAP." Anyone have any idea what we mean by that acronym, GAAP? Yes, Susan?

F1: Um, I think it means "Generally Accepted Accounting Practices."

M2: Almost right. Anyone else? Michael?

M1: Generally Accepted Accounting *Principles*, I think.

M2: Bingo, you got it. Today we're going to talk about three of the most important of these principles. First, the business entity principle. Who can explain that principle—Elaine?

F2: Uh, it means that a business has to keep its accounts separate from its owner's account. Is that right?

M2: Indeed it is, Elaine. It means an owner's assets and liabilities are not the same as his or her business's assets and liabilities. Now, another principle we're going to consider today is the cost principle. Michael, what do you think that might be?

M1: I don't know, professor—does it mean that costs always have to be recorded in the books?

M2: Well, not just that they have to be recorded, but that they have to be recorded at the price at which they were originally purchased—*not* at today's market value. Let's say you bought 10 computers five years ago for $1,000 each, and that today they are worth half that. This principle says that you have to keep them on your books as being worth $1,000. We'll talk more about this later, but first I want to mention the last principle we'll consider today, which is the matching principle. Anyone know what that is? Susan?

F1: No idea, Professor.

M1: Anyone else? No? Well, this principle simply states that a firm has to record any expenses it incurs while selling goods or services in the period when the sale was made. If you own a used car lot and your books say you sold a car in December, you have to record the expense of the salesperson's December salary along with that sale. Okay, we're going to go back and talk about all these principles in more detail, but before we do that, does anyone have any questions?

3. Match the accounting principle with the appropriate description of it.

F2: You will hear part of a guest lecture given in a class in agronomy. The lecture focuses on locally grown crops.

M1: Hello, I'm Floyd Haney. I'm the U.S. Department of Agriculture's county agent here in Harrison County. Professor Mackenzie asked me to talk to you about the agricultural situation in Harrison County today. Now, you probably already know that our main crop is traditionally wheat, followed by corn. Wheat is still the most important but, did you realize that, in the last few years, soy beans have become considerably more important economically than corn? I'll bet that's a surprise for most of you. Then, of course, in the southern part of the county, there are a number of organic fruit farms, mostly growing apples and pears, but so far, these are not nearly as important to our county economically as any of the three crops I mentioned.

So let's talk about our top crop, which is wheat, as I said. According to the U.S. Department of Agriculture, there are seven types of wheat, depending on their texture and color. You'll find three or four of those growing here in Harrison County. You get a lot of durum wheat here, which is mainly used for making pasta—spaghetti, macaroni, and so on. Then there's soft white wheat, which is generally purchased by companies that make breakfast cereals. And of course, you have hard red wheat, which makes wonderful bread flour.

4. The lecturer mentions four types of crops that are grown in Harrison County. Rank these four crops in their order of economic importance, beginning with the MOST important.

5. Match the type of wheat with the product that is most often made from it.

F2: Listen to part of a discussion in a history class. The class has been focusing on the history of exploration.

M1: Okay, we're going to go on with our discussion of explorers and exploration. Today we're talking about twentieth century explorers. You know, usually, when we talk about explorers in the twentieth century, we think of space explorers walking on the Moon. But in the early part of the century, the most important sphere of discovery was Antarctica. Tell me, has anyone here ever read anything about the early exploration of Antarctica?

F1: When I was in high school, I read a book by Admiral Byrd called *Alone*, about the winter he spent in a shelter in Antarctica by himself.

M1: Yes, that's a fascinating book.

F1: I was amazed at how he could survive in that terrible cold, dark shelter all winter by himself.

M2: Professor Smith, was Byrd the first person to get to the South Pole?

M1: No, he was the first person to fly over the South Pole, in 1929, but not the first person to go there on foot. In 1929 he also established the first large-scale camp in Antarctica. Since he was from the United States, he named it Little America.

M2: So who was the first to the South Pole, then?

M1: That's an interesting question. About twenty years before Byrd's flight, there was something of a race to get to the South Pole by foot. It was a little like the space race in the 50s and 60s. The first explorer to get *near* the South Pole was a British explorer, named Shackleton. That was in 1909. He was less than a hundred miles from the Pole when he had to turn around.

M2: Why did he turn back when he was so close?

M1: Well, he was running low on supplies, and, as so often happens in Antarctica, the weather turned bad. Then in 1911, two expeditions headed for the Pole. The first one to leave was under the Norwegian explorer Roald Amundson, the other was under another British explorer, Robert Scott.

F1: Don't keep us in suspense—who won?

M1: Amundson's party reached the Pole in December of 1911. Scott's party got there about a month later, in January of 1912.

F1: Oh, the people in Scott's party must have been terribly disappointed.

M2: Yes, apparently they were very discouraged, and the return trip to their base turned into a nightmare. They suffered setback after setback, then, of course, terrible storms came up, and none of them survived the trip.

6. The professor discusses some of the history of Antarctic exploration. Summarize this history by putting these expeditions in the order in which they began.

7. Match these Antarctic explorers with the countries from which they came.

F1: Listen to a lecture in a musical acoustics class about decibel levels.

F2: Sound levels below about 40 decibels are not very useful in music. They require that background noise, such as audience movement or ventilating systems, be even lower—and that often is not the case. Levels over about 100 are not only unpleasantly loud but also can be damaging to the ear. As a matter of fact, lately I've been doing a little research on my own on decibel levels that I want to share with you. Last week I went to an amplified rock concert by a band called the Creatures—at least, I think that's what they were called—and I took a sound-level meter with me. I measured sound levels as high as 115 decibels from my seat. Oh, and I can vouch for the fact that this level of sound is painfully loud! A couple of nights later, I measured the sound levels at a concert by the Metropolitan Philharmonic Symphony. Although a full orchestra is theoretically capable of producing sounds at a much higher level, I didn't record any sounds from my seat above 90 decibels. Most of the sound levels were much lower. And when the first violinist performed a solo, the highest level I detected was around only 60 decibels.

8. Match the performance with its maximum decibel level.

F2: You will hear part of a lecture in a U.S. literature class. The class has been discussing American writers of the nineteenth century.

F1: Well, I told you at the end of the last class that I thought you would enjoy the reading assignment that I gave you—was I right? (*Pause*) Yes, I thought so . . . . most students like reading the works of Edgar Allen Poe—maybe because so many of them have been turned into spooky movies!

Let's take a brief look at Poe's early life. He was born in Boston in 1809. He was orphaned at an early age and was adopted by a businessman, John Allen. He was taken by Allen to England when he was six, and went to private school there. He returned to the United States in 1820 and enrolled for one year at the University of Virginia. However, his adoptive father was displeased with him for drinking and gambling too much, and forced him to quit school and take a job as a clerk.

As you might imagine, the young, artistic Poe hated this job. He soon quit and wrote his first book of poems. Shortly after, he reconciled with John Allen, who got him an appointment at West Point, the U.S. military academy. However, Poe didn't do well at the academy either, and he was thrown out after only a few months for neglecting his duties. After that, his foster father disowned him permanently. Now, I'll talk about the rest of Poe's life later, after we've had a chance to discuss some of his works, because the tragic events of the latter part of his life deeply influenced the mood and the tone of his works. Poe's first love was poetry. He considered himself primarily a poet and said that he wrote other works mainly to make money. The poem I asked you to read was "The Raven," one of his most famous. Isn't it amazing how he creates such a sad and mysterious and downright scary mood in that poem? I also asked you to read his horror story, "The Fall of the House of Usher." Again, the mood is gloomy and haunting, but the plot and characterization is outstanding. Finally, you read "The Gold Bug." Poe basically invented the detective story and this is one of his finest. Okay, everyone take out your book and open to page 174. I'm going to read the poem "The Raven" aloud, and I want you to pay particular attention to the rhythm and to the sound of Poe's words.

9. The professor gives a brief biography of the writer Edgar Allen Poe. List these events from his life in the order in which they occurred.

10. Match these works by Edgar Allen Poe with the type of writing that they represent.

Review Test C: Longer Talks

Answer Key

1. To look up some terms.
2. Some index cards.
3. The part of the library where books are shelved.
4. To discuss the domestication of dogs. / To describe the various tasks dogs have been given.
5. By selective breeding.
6. The remains of an early specimen of a domesticated dog were found there.
7. (D), (A), (B), (C)
8. (B)
9. It would not involve any work for students interested in costumes and scenery.
10. (A), (C), (B)
11. In the seventeenth century.
12. *The Crucible*.
13. Get a book.
14. It has the highest tuition rates in the state.
15. The president of the Student Council.
16. The proposal to increase student services will not be adopted.
17. During the Revolutionary War.
18. His dictionary.
19. A spelling book.
20. F-O-T-O-G-R-A-F instead of P-H-O-T-O-G-R-A-P-H. / N-I-F instead of K-N-I-F-E.

Audio Script

M2: Listen to a conversation at a university library.

M1: Hi, Martha. What brings you to the library?

F2: Oh, I just came to look up some terms in the *Encyclopedia of Art* for my art history class. What about you, Stanley?

M1: I've got two papers due at the end of this term, and I've been getting an early start on them by collecting some references and writing down some statistics. I've spent most of the day here.

F2: Really? Well, you ought to be ready for a break them. Want to go get a snack or something?

M1: You know, that sounds great—let me just get my things together and . . . hey, where are my notes?

F2: What notes?

M1: The notes I spent all day working on. I don't see them.

F2: You mean you lost your notebook?

M1: No, I don't use a notebook—I take notes on index cards.

F2: Well, just think about where you could have left them. Re-trace your steps since you came in the library.

M1: Let's see—when I first arrived, I came here, to the reference room.

F2: Maybe they're somewhere in this room, then.

M1: No, I had them after that. I went to the stacks next . . .

F2: Stacks? What do you mean, the stacks?

M1: You know, the book stacks. That's what they call the main part of the library, where most of the books are shelved.

F2: Well, that's where you should look.

M1: No, after that I went up to look at some journals in the periodicals room up on the third floor, and I remember having them up there. I'll bet that's where they are.

F2: Well, you go look up there, and I'll check with one of the librarians behind the main desk, just in case someone turned them in.

M1: Okay, and thanks for helping me out. Just as soon as I find my note cards, we'll go get a bite to eat.

1. Why did Martha come to the library?
2. What did Stanley lose?
3. According to Stanley, what does the term "stacks" refer to?

M2: Listen to a lecture in an anthropology class. The class has been discussing the domestication of animals.

F1: All right, class, last week we talked about the process of domesticating animals in general. Today, we're going to talk in some detail about the first animal to be domesticated—the dog.

No one knows when or where the dog was first domesticated. It's believed, however, that the process took place more than 10,000 years ago. The remains of what is thought to be an early example of a domesticated dog was found in a cave in Idaho. These remains are believed to be around 10,500 years old. So, domestication took place during humankind's earliest stage of development—the hunter-gatherer period.

All of the dogs you see today, from Chihuahuas to Great Danes, are descendants of wolves. Obviously, domestication of these wild creatures required that humans select the most useful and easily trained young animals as breeding stock. As such selection continued over countless generations, dogs became adapted to many tasks.

Dogs apparently first served as guards. With their keen sense of smell and hearing, dogs made it almost impossible for strangers to approach a sleeping village by surprise. And later, humans took advantage of dogs' hunting instincts. Dogs learned to help humans procure meat and skins from wild animals. Then, after humans domesticated herd animals such as goats, cattle, and sheep, dogs helped round these herd animals up and move them from place to place by barking and nipping at their heels.

Take a look at this fresco from the wall of a sandstone grotto in the Sahara. It's probably about 5,000 years old. The herders are driving their oxen home from the field, while their "best friend" is apparently helping them.

Of course, after that, at some unknown time, dogs began to take on a new role, the role that most of them have today. They began to be valued not so much for the work they did as for the company they provided.

4. What are the main purposes of the lecture?
5. According to the lecturer, how did early humans adapt dogs to different tasks?
6. Why does the lecturer mention Idaho?
7. The lecturer mentions a number of roles that dogs have played since they were first domesticated. List these roles in the correct chronological order.
8. Click on the part of the picture that represents the herders' "best friend."

M2: Listen to a discussion in a drama class. The class is trying to decide which play they will stage.

F2: In the next few days we have to chose a play to put on in the spring.

F1: I have an idea, Professor Kemp. How about Thornton Wilder's play *Our Town*. My senior class put that on when I was in high school. I thought it was a really interesting play.

F2: That's a good idea, Lynn, but that play is usually performed without any costumes or any kind of elaborate scenery, and I would like the students interested in costume and scenery design to have a chance to show off their talents as well as the actors. Any other ideas? Yes, Larry?

M1: Suppose we did a musical, like A *Chorus Line*?

F2: That would be a lot of fun. But I'm afraid I wouldn't be able to direct a musical—I just don't have the experience or the musical background myself.

F1: I've always loved Shakespeare—we could put on one of his comedies, like *The Tempest*.

F2: I love Shakespeare myself, and that's tempting. The only problem is that, every summer, the university has a Shakespeare festival and puts on three Shakespearean plays at the amphitheater on campus. I don't really want it to seem like our spring production is in competition with the festival in any way.

M1: How about Arthur Miller's play, *The Crucible*? I saw a version of that play on television a few months ago, and I was really impressed.

F2: Ummm. . . . *The Crucible*. I think you might be on to something there, Larry. That's an excellent choice. Anyone else have an opinion on that play?

F1: Tell you the truth, I've never seen it or read it. What's it about?

F2: Well, it takes place in the late seventeenth century, and it's about the Salem Witch Trials.

F1: Oh, I studied those in history class. A lot of innocent women were persecuted because people thought they were witches, right?

F2: Right, Lynn. In a broader sense, its really about any group that persecutes a minority because they are afraid of them. Arthur Miller wrote this play in the 1950s, which was the early part of the Cold War. At the time, the Congress was investigating dissidents in the United States. In fact, Miller himself was investigated. So, the witch trials are a kind of metaphor for that investigation.

F1: Well, I think it sounds like a good choice . . . it's not only a period play, but it's also a play that has a contemporary message.

F2: I'll tell you what . . . I'd like everyone to get hold of a copy of *The Crucible*, either from the bookstore or the library, and take a look at it, and the next time class meets, we'll make a final decision.

9. Why does Professor Kemp NOT want to stage the play *Our Town* this spring?
10. Professor Kemp and her students discuss a number of plays. Match the characteristics of the play with the title of the play.
11. In what time period is the play *The Crucible* set?
12. Which of these plays does Professor Kemp show the most enthusiasm for staging?
13. What does Professor Kemp ask the students to do before their next class?

M2: Listen to a conversation between two students.

M1: Hi Nicole, what are you reading?

F1: Just the campus paper. Hey, did you see the lead story?

M1: No, I didn't. What's going on?

F1: The Board of Regents voted to raise tuition again here at Babcock University next year. Can you believe it?

M1: Again? This is the third year in a row, isn't it? We must be attending the most expensive university in the state now.

F1: According to the article, only Hambleton College is more expensive.

M1: So, does the article say what the university is going to use this money for? I hope they plan to replace some of the computers in the computer labs. A lot of them are ancient.

F1: Well, here, I'll read what it says about that: "Student Council president Penny Chang asked the Board of Regents for a corresponding increase in student services, such as longer hours at the library and more contact time with faculty. But a spokesperson for the administration said that the money has already been earmarked for higher insurance premiums that the university is being charged and for the construction of a new addition to one of the dormitories, Nevin Hall."

M1: Well—I'm glad I have only one more semester to go. Otherwise, I just couldn't afford to go to school here.

14. What does the article that Nicole is reading say about Hambleton College?
15. Who is Penny Chang?
16. What can be inferred from the remark made by the spokesperson for the administration?

M2: Listen to a lecture in a linguistics class. The class has been discussing the differences between American English and British English.

M1: Today I'm going to talk a little about Noah Webster and the impact he had on American English. Webster was born in Connecticut in 1758 and graduated from Yale University in 1778, during the American Revolution. Right after graduation, Webster joined George Washington's army to fight against the British. The end of the war brought independence from Britain for the thirteen colonies, but political independence alone didn't satisfy Webster. He wanted the former colonies to be intellectually independent from Britain as well.

In 1783 Webster published a spelling book which would become known to generations of schoolchildren as the "blue-backed book" because of its blue cover. A couple of years later, he published his dictionary. It is for his dictionary that Webster is chiefly remembered today. The *Webster's Dictionary* popular today is a direct descendant of that book published in the 1780s.

In his dictionary, Webster made many changes in the way English was used in the United States. He suggested new ways of pronouncing words and added words used only in the former colonies to the language. Most of the changes, though, involved spelling. Today, most people in the United States spell certain words differently from people in Britain because of Webster's original dictionary. Let me just give you a couple of examples—in Britain, words like *center* end in R-E. In the United States, these words end in E-R because that's how they were spelled in Webster's dictionary. Webster also took out the letter U from words like *color*. In the British spelling, that word ends with the letters O-U-R, but in the American spelling, it ends with O-R..

Still, Webster did not go as far in revising spelling as his friend Benjamin Franklin wanted him to. Franklin wanted to drop all silent letters from words. The word *wrong* would have been spelled R-O-N-G, and the word *lamb* would have been L-A-M.

17. According to the speaker, when did Webster graduate from Yale University?

18. What is Noah Webster mainly remembered for today?

19. According to the speaker, what kind of book was the "blue-backed book?"

20. Which of the following are spellings that Benjamin Franklin would probably have approved of?

Mini-Lessons for Section 1

Mini-Lesson 1.1

1. about to
2. at the drop of a hat
3. Beats me
4. broke in on
5. better off
6. As a rule
7. broke down
8. a breeze
9. bound to
10. brought up

11. by and large
12. add up
13. be my guest
14. by heart
15. bring . . . up
16. break up
17. at ease
18. break the ice
19. brush up on
20. bit off more than . . . can chew

Mini-Lesson 1.2   4 2CH

1. called off
2. calm down
3. came across
4. count on
5. come up with
6. checked into / checked out
7. checked . . . out of
8. call it a day
9. chip in
10. cut off
11. clear up
12. come around to
13. cost an arm and a leg
14. care for
15. Cheer up
16. caught up with
17. cut out for
18. catch on

Mini-Lesson 1.3   X 2CH

1. figure out
2. eyes . . . bigger than . . . stomach
3. dreamed up
4. feel like
5. fallen behind
6. few and far between
7. Feel free
8. fed up with
9. drop . . . a line
10. a far cry from
11. drop out of
12. died down
13. drop in on
14. day in and day out
15. dwell on

Mini-Lesson 1.4   X 4CH

1. gotten in touch with
2. fill out
3. fill in
4. gave . . . the cold shoulder
5. for good / for the time being
6. get rid of
7. give away
8. a fish out of water
9. get a kick out of
10. got on
11. get off the ground
12. get along with
13. filled in for
14. get under way
15. get off

Mini-Lesson 1.5   4 3CH

1. grew up
2. handed out / handed in
3. hit the road
4. have a word with
5. go on with
6. Hold still
7. go easy on
8. go . . . with
9. had a chip on . . . shoulder
10. went overboard
11. gave . . . hand
12. goes without saying
13. held up
14. heard from / having the time of . . . life
15. give . . . a hand with
16. hard to come by

Mini-Lesson 1.6   ✗ 2CH

1. keep an eye on
2. keeping up with
3. learned the ropes
4. in a nutshell
5. jump to conclusions
6. keep an eye out for
7. in the long run
8. left out
9. in no time
10. kill . . . time

11. let up
12. in the same boat
13. keep on
14. leave . . . alone
15. know . . . like the back of . . . hand
16. keep track of
17. in the dark
18. in store
19. iron out
20. in hot water

Mini-Lesson 1.7   ✗ 5ch

1. an old hand at
2. on second thought
3. make . . . up
4. Out of order
5. looks up to
6. on hand
7. make sense of
8. make a point of / over and over
9. on the tip of . . . tongue
10. out of the question
11. out of
12. music to . . . ears
13. on end

14. odds and ends
15. on the go
16. make up . . . mind
17. mixed up
18. on pins and needles
19. look . . . up
20. make way for
21. next to nothing
22. on. . . . own
23. No harm done
24. out of . . . mind
25. over . . . head

Mini-Lesson 1.8   ✗ 2ch

1. put up with
2. a pretty penny / picked up the tab for
3. pat . . . on the back
4. play . . . .by ear
5. part with
6. picked . . . up
7. put . . . on
8. put together

9. passed . . . with flying colors
10. Pay attention
11. pulling . . . leg
12. picked up / put . . . away
13. put off
14. picked out
15. pass . . . up

Mini-Lesson 1.9   4ch

1. saw . . . off
2. short for
3. ran out of
4. right away
5. snowed under
6. sign up for
7. So far, so good
8. ring a bell with
9. spell . . . out for
10. run of the mill
11. singing another tune
12. rough it
13. show up
14. run for office
15. sleep on it
16. running a temperature
17. Save your breath
18. see eye to eye with . . . on
19. ran into
20. slowly but surely

Mini-Lesson 1.10   2ch

1. stamp out
2. stay up
3. stay out
4. take after
5. taking apart
6. a stone's throw from
7. stand for
8. stuck with
9. takes a lot of nerve
10. Stick with
11. spick-and-span
12. stood out
13. stack up against
14. stand for
15. straighten up / stop by
16. take advantage of
17. stock up on

Mini-Lesson 1.11   9ch brozne !

1. try on
2. talked . . . into
3. tore up
4. tell . . . apart
5. take up
6. took a short cut
7. taking off
8. tear . . . away from
9. throw the book at
10. Take off
11. tried out
12. talked . . . out of
13. try out for / take the plunge
14. throw away

Mini-Lesson 1.12

1. turns into or turned into
2. Turn off
3. turn down
4. turn up
5. turn on
6. worn out
7. warm up
8. turned out (or turned up)
9. turn in
10. what the doctor ordered
11. without a hitch
12. work out
13. watch out
14. Turn around
15. worked . . . out
16. wait on
17. turned . . . down
18. warm up
19. walking on air
20. under the weather

Preview Test 2

Answer		Explanation
1.	one	The only choice that correctly completes this sentence is an appositive.
2.	thousand	The plural verb *are* indicates that a plural subject, *thousands*, must be used.
3.	or	The correct pattern is *neither . . . nor*.
4.	have	A verb is required to complete the sentence.
5.	it was	The use of the pronoun subject *it* is unnecessary; *it* should be omitted.
6.	analysis of stars	For parallelism, a noun phrase is required.
7.	most old	The superlative form of a one-syllable adjective (*old*) is formed with the suffix *-est*: *oldest*.
8.	which in	The preposition must precede the relative pronoun: *in which*.
9.	are	The subject of the clause (*one species*) is singular, so the singular verb *is* must be used.
10.	as gold	The correct way to complete this comparison is by completing the *as* + adjective + *as* phrase (*as pliable as gold.*)
11.	obtained	The only correct way to complete this sentence is with a participle (*obtained* really means *which is obtained*).
12.	engineer	In order to be parallel with the other words in the series (*logic* and *probability*) the name of the field (*engineering*) must be used.
13.	no	The adjective *no* is needed before the noun phrase *federal laws*.
14.	potential	An adverb (*potentially*), not an adjective (*potential*), is needed.
15.	Through	This sentence can be correctly completed only with an introductory prepositional phrase (*through experimental studies*).
16.	Despite	*Despite* is only used before noun phrases. An adverb-clause marker (*although*) must be used with a clause.
17.	injure	A noun (*injury*), not a verb (*injure*), is required.
18.	the Statue of Liberty was given to the to the United States by the people of France	This is the only subject of the sentence that logically goes with the modifier, *Designed by . . .*

Answer	Explanation
19. both of which	This choice correctly follows the pattern quantifier + *of* + relative pronoun.
20. Although	This sentence can be completed correctly only with an adverb clause introduced by the marker *Although*. (*Even though* would also be correct.)
21. That diamonds	This sentence can be completed correctly only with an noun clause introduced by the marker *That*.
22. <u>that</u>	The pronoun refers to a plural noun phrase (*public buildings*) so the plural pronoun *those* must be used.
23. are botanical gardens	A main verb such as *are* is required to complete the clause (*to be* is not a main verb), and the subject and verb must be inverted because the clause begins with the negative phrase *not only*.
24. <u>Since</u>	The verb in this sentence is in the past tense to indicate that something occurred at a specific time in the past. The preposition *In* should therefore replace *Since*. *Since* is used with the present perfect tense.
25. <u>believe</u>	The noun *belief* should be used in place of the verb *believe*.

Structure Lessons and Review Tests

Note: Items marked with an asterisk (*) do not focus on the structures that are presented in that lesson. Corrections for error identification items appear in parentheses after the answer.

Exercise 13

1. water treatment
2. is one method
3. Canada adopted
4. It is
5. Harvard University has
6. became famous
7. There are two
*8. That Philip Glass
9. The Earth is constantly bombarded
10. The three

11. It was Jane Byrne
*12. that work
13. there is no
14. are covered
15. it is difficult
16. was James Fenimore Cooper
17. The first
18. the California poppy grows
19. they
20. It was in 1790

Exercise 14

1. that
*2. became
3. which with (with which)
4. where engineers were educated
5. whom (which)
6. which (who)
7. that are cultivated in the United States
8. whose novels describe
9. which resemble
*10. become (became)
*11. but they
12. their (whose)
13. the pilot must watch
14. whose
15. they are (that are)
16. use them (use)
17. for which it is
*18. band (bands)
19. that touches
20. that they (that)
21. who wrote
*22. informations (information)
23. firefighters who
24. most of which
25. is *Women and Economics*, in which

Exercise 15

1. if
2. Even though
3. Despite (Although)
4. When
5. Because of (Because)
*6. their (its)
7. Since
8. As a wave rolls
9. because of (because)
*10. Today
11. Whenever people live
12. Although
13. because (because of)
14. During (When)
15. Until they have been cooked
*16. politics (politicians)
17. in spite of the availability of
*18. everywhere
19. Since (Because of)
20. When shone
21. However
*22. weigh (weight)
*23. The reason that
24. Once a patent is
25. While

Exercise 16

1. That raindrops
2. how fleas are
3. that Anna Winlock
4. are they (they are)
5. What ecologists call a "gallery forest"

*6. Heavy industry

7. What makes the monarch butterflies' migration

8. <u>are the qualities</u> (the qualities are)

9. what the requirements for each vegetable are

10. <u>was the wheel</u> (the wheel was)

11. whether life

*12. <u>clearly</u> (clear)

13. That the ancestor

*14. If

15. that

Exercise 17.1

1. C

2. X the quality of the water (*or* the water quality)

3. C

4. X warm

5. X stories

6. C

7. X grinding

8. X religion

9. X heat

10. X a critic

11. X is inexpensive

12. X control floods

Exercise 17.2

1. <u>and mountain</u> (and on mountain)

2. conditioning soil

3. <u>adjustment</u> (adjust)

4. <u>boiling</u> (boiled)

5. frozen

6. handled easily

7. <u>history</u> (historic)

8. the founder of

9. <u>and specialized</u> (and more specialized)

10. brushes

11. <u>to have economic</u> (economic)

12. in offices

13. resulted in an exchange of ideas

14. <u>packaging</u> (package)

15. <u>loyally</u> (loyal)

16. <u>playing a game</u> (a game)

17. how much money

*18. serving

19. <u>vegetables</u> (vegetable)

20. <u>a design</u> (a designer)

*21. <u>has</u> (have)

22. administrative center

23. <u>economic</u> (economics)

24. <u>hear</u> (hearing *or* sound)

25. provided easy credit

Review Test D: Structure

Answer	Explanation
1. The vacuum milking machine was invented	This choice correctly supplies a subject and a verb.
2. by which	The correct pattern is preposition + adjective clause marker.
3. <u>that resemble</u>	The adjective clause marker *that* is not needed and should be omitted.
4. when the work	The adverb clause marker *when* and the subject of the adverb clause *the work* are missing.
5. <u>Despite</u>	*Despite* is only used before noun phrases; before a clause an adverb clause marker such as *although* is needed.
6. <u>colorful</u>	The noun *color* is needed for parallelism.
7. That all deserts	Only a noun clause can correctly complete this sentence.
8. prevent	The verb *prevent* is needed for parallelism.
9. If two	An adverb clause is required to complete this sentence correctly.
10. There are many	This is the only choice that supplies the missing main verb.
11. <u>safety</u>	The adjective *safe* is needed for parallelism.
12. <u>that</u>	The adjective clause marker *that* cannot introduce an identifying (restrictive) adjective clause (one that is set off by commas); the marker *which* should be used instead.
13. a musician	A noun phrase is required for parallelism.
14. Although	This sentence can be correctly completed with a reduced adverb clause.
15. <u>because their</u>	The expression *because of* must be used in place of *because* before a noun phrase.
16. It takes	The only way to complete this sentence is with the pattern It *takes* + time expression + *for* someone /something + infinitive.
17. one of which,	This choice correctly follows the pattern quantifier + *of* + adjective clause marker.
18. <u>uses it</u>	The object pronoun *it* is used unnecessarily in this clause; the relative pronoun *which* is the object of the clause.
19. What psychologists call cognition	A noun clause is required to complete the sentence; the first choice incorrectly uses direct question word order.
20. <u>superstitious</u>	The noun *superstitions* is needed for parallelism.

Exercise 18.1

1. differ	difference		differently
2.	competition (*or* competitiveness)	competitive	competitively
3. deepen	depth	deep	
4. decide		decisive (*or* decided)	decisively (*or* decidedly)
5.	beauty (*or* beautification)	beautiful	beautifully
6.	prohibition	prohibitive (*or* prohibited)	prohibitively
7. emphasize	emphasis		emphatically
8. inconvenience	inconvenience		inconveniently
9. glorify (*or* glory)		glorious	gloriously
10.	mystery (*or* mystification)	mysterious	mysteriously
11. generalize	generality (*or* generalization)		generally
12. simplify	simplicity (*or* simplification)	simple	
13. purify	purity (*or* purification)		purely
14.	freedom	free (*or* freed)	freely
15.	restriction	restrictive (*or* restricted)	restrictively

Exercise 18.2

1.	musician	musical
2. surgery		surgical
3. poetry	poet	
4. technology		technological (*or* technical)
5.	administrator	administrative
6. finance	financier	
7. photography		photographic
8.	theoretician (*or* theorist)	theoretical (*or* theoretic)
9. athletics	athlete	
10.	grammarian	grammatical
11. philosophy		philosophical (*or* philosophic)
12. crime		criminal
13. politics	politician	
14. law		legal
15.	humorist	humorous

Exercise 18.3

1. greatly
2. annually
3. Regular
4. simple
5. beautiful
6. Generally / simple
7. permanently
8. widely
9. close
10. easy
11. incredible
12. automatically
13. formal
14. commercially
15. masterful / deeply

Exercise 18.4

1. fictional (Adj)
2. industry (N) / products (N)
3. fragrant (Adj)
4. mathematical (Adj) / equal (Adj)
5. severity (N)
6. development (N)
7. differ (V) / originate (V)
8. magician (PN)
9. depth (N)
10. distinction (N) / perfectly (Adv)
11. scholarly (Adj) / immigration (N)
12. food (N) / rainy (Adj)
13. symbolize (V) / occupation (N)
14. relieve (V)
15. member (PN) / interpreter (PN)
16. outer (Adj) / constantly (Adv)
17. tropical (Adj) / ability (N)
18. lose (V) / rapidly (Adv)
19. ripen (V)
20. painstakingly (Adv) / grammar (N) / factual (Adj)

Exercise 18.5

1. intellectually (intellectual)
2. destruction (destructive)
3. important (importance)
4. analysis (analyzes)
5. dancers (dances)
6. strong (strength)
7. weigh (weight)
*8. purpose (purposes)
9. farms (farming)
10. good (well)
11. measuring (measurement, measure)
12. literary (literature)
13. react (reaction)
14. sharp (sharpness)
15. live (life)
16. healthy (health)
17. neighbors (neighborhoods)
*18. exposed of (exposed to)
19. success (successful)
20. collect (collection)
*21. to (and)
22. lucky (luck)
23. absent (absence)
24. politics (politicians)
25. hard (harden)

Exercise 19.1

1. made	3. made	5. did	7. made	9. do
2. done	4. do	6. make	8. make	10. make

Exercise 19.2

1. so	3. So	5. too	7. such a	9. too
2. too	4. such a	6. as	8. so	10. such

Exercise 19.3

1. another	4. another	7. other	10. another
2. other	5. other	8. Other	11. another
3. other	6. another	9. other	12. other

Exercise 19.4

1. Many	3. much	5. number	7. amounts	9. Many
2. little	4. few	6. little	8. many	10. little

Exercise 19.5

1. before	6. earliest	11. near	16. most
2. twice	7. round	12. live	17. Almost
3. afterwards	8. somewhat	13. percent	18. tell
4. Most	9. tell	14. old	19. nearly
5. age	10. never	15. after	20. ever

Exercise 19.6

1. <u>an alive</u> (a live)
2. <u>so much</u> (as much)
3. <u>near</u> (nearly)
4. <u>age</u> (of age, *or* old)
5. <u>few</u> (little)
6. <u>ever</u> (never)

*7. <u>symbolize</u> (symbol)
8. <u>making</u> (doing)
9. <u>another</u> (other)
10. <u>amount</u> (number)
*11. <u>are</u> (is)
12. <u>soonest</u> (earliest)

Exercise 20.1

1. is
2. was
3. are
4. was
5. is
6. are
7. are
8. was
9. makes
10. are
11. is
12. varies
13. are
14. was
15. goes

Exercise 20.2

1. X shipped
2. X was built
3. X is known
4. X worn
5. X has been growing (*or* has grown)
6. X does
7. X are played
8. X was
9. X came
10. C
11. X ran
12. C
13. X were chosen
14. X have used
15. X were produced

Exercise 20.3

1. <u>to study</u> (study)
2. founded
3. <u>have lived</u> (lived)
4. flew
5. <u>does</u> (do)
6. contain
7. wrote
8. <u>require</u> (requires)
9. <u>spin</u> (spun)
10. <u>ate</u> (eat)
11. feed
12. is used
*13. <u>tooth</u> (teeth)
14. has been held
*15. to soak
16. <u>did</u> (was)
17. <u>describes</u> (described)
18. build
19. <u>shaking</u> (shaken)
20. became
*21. <u>lived now</u> (living now)
22. <u>dip</u> (dipped)
23. was
24. have
25. installed

Exercise 21.1

1. known
2. astonishing
3. written
4. twisting
5. working
6. filled
7. named
8. appearing
9. deposited
10. regarded

Exercise 21.2

1. acting
2. <u>mixing</u> (mixed)
3. Plants grown
4. Produced by the fermentation of organic matter
5. <u>were silhouetted</u> (silhouetted)
6. houses dating
*7. <u>40 mile</u> (40 miles)
8. patterned
9. <u>crushing</u> (crushed)
10. A filter placed
11. which was completed
12. <u>cracking</u> (cracked)
*13. is known

*14. <u>the</u> (his)
15. making important discoveries
16. concerned with
17. Receiving
18. <u>stimulated</u> (stimulating)
19. <u>holding</u> (held)
*20. appear

Exercise 22.1

1. to control
2. move
3. producing
4. to have
5. to grow
6. to catch
7. to communicate
8. bringing
9. to bend
10. miss
11. to snap
12. to rupture
13. to describe
14. to be awarded
15. achieving

Exercise 22.2

1. <u>package</u> (packaging)
2. Training
3. to appear
4. <u>to cutting</u> (to cut)
5. <u>to classify</u> (classifying)
*6. protects
7. to avoid
*8. <u>obtaining</u> (obtained)
9. by passing
10. To develop film
*11. <u>another</u> (other)
12. to determine the costs
13. Crossing rivers
14. <u>to sparkle</u> (sparkle)
15. <u>Bathe</u> (Bathing)
16. to do work
17. binding books
18. <u>for play</u> (to play)
19. To operate, corporations
20. gripping
21. <u>to smoke</u> (smoking)
22. used to power
*23. have
24. <u>catching</u> (to catch)
25. to be established

Review Test E

Answer	Explanation
1. To survive	Of the four choices, only an infinitive correctly completes the sentence.
2. <u>difference</u>	The adjective form *different* is needed in place of the noun *difference*.
3. skaters to maintain	After the verb *allow*, an infinitive is required.
4. <u>playing</u>	The past participle *played* is used to form the present perfect tense.
5. been held	This is the correct way to form the present perfect passive verb.
6. <u>done</u>	The word *made* is required; it means *manufactured*.
7. <u>alike</u>	The correct pattern is A, *like* B, *is* . . .
8. Planting trees	Only a gerund phrase correctly completes this sentence.
9. <u>numbers</u>	Before an uncountable noun (*food*), *amounts* must be used in place of *numbers*.
10. <u>Lightly</u>	The adjective *Light* should be used in place of the adverb.
11. became	A main verb in the past tense is needed to complete the sentence.
12. <u>were giving</u>	To form the passive verb required here, a past participle (*given*) must be used in place of the *-ing* form.
13. built	A past participle (meaning *which are built*)is needed here.
14. <u>approaching</u>	After the verb *permit*, the infinitive *to approach* must be used.
15. <u>spice</u>	The adjective *spicy* is needed in place of the noun.
16. substance formed	A noun + participle is the best answer here: this phrase means *a substance which was formed*.
17. <u>to teaching</u>	This is the wrong form of the infinitive; the correct form is *to teach*.
18. <u>writing</u>	The past participle *written* is required to convey a passive meaning.
19. <u>to walk</u>	After the verb *let*, the simple form of the verb (*walk*) is required.
20. <u>send</u>	The past participle *sent* is needed in the formation of the passive modal verb.
21. concentrating	A present participle correctly completes this sentence; it means *which concentrates* and has an active meaning.
22. <u>so</u>	Before an adjective + noun (*high degree*) *such a* must be used.
23. <u>soonest</u>	The correct word choice is *earliest*.
24. <u>various</u>	The noun *variety* should be used.
25. <u>photograph</u>	The gerund *photographing* is needed after a preposition.

Section 2: Structure

Exercise 23.1

1. X its
2. X it
3. X it
4. C
5. X its
6. X it
7. C
8. X those
9. X their
10. X its
11. X their
12. X that

Exercise 23.2

1. X her
2. X them
3. C
4. X our
5. X themselves
6. C
7. X his
8. X its
9. X themselves
10. X they

Exercise 23.3

1. its (their)
2. they are (are)
3. themselves (them)
4. these (those)
5. them (themselves)
6. she helped (helped)
*7. Almost (Most)
8. its (their)
9. their (its)
10. they are (are)
11. himself (itself)
12. that (this)
*13. recover (to recover)
*14. photographers (photographs)
15. it was (was)

Exercise 24

1. mammal (mammals)
2. humans (human)
3. automobiles (automobile)
4. years (year)
5. source (sources)
6. percents (percent)
7. All college (All colleges)
8. thousand (thousands)
9. 500-pages (500-page)
10. man (men)
11. underwriter (underwriters)
12. appliance (appliances)
13. foot (feet)
*14. growth (grown)
15. farms (farm)
16. medicines (medicine)
*17. more (most)
18. woman (women)
19. trillions (trillion)
20. sunlights (sunlight)

Exercise 25.1

1. in   on   of
2. For   against   within   of
3. of   to   since   into
4. At   of   of   along   between
5. of   in   of   on   in
6. at   on   to   of
7. of   on   by   with   on
8. off   of   for   of
9. In   for   from   to
10. In   at   to   on
11. In   on   of   of   at
12. to   of   by   in   of   in
13. In   of   by   of   in   through
14. on   of   to   on
15. in   for   of   in   since

Exercise 25.2

1. O <u>According polls</u>   to
2. O <u>thanks improved</u>   to
3. C
4. I <u>of</u>
5. I <u>on</u>
6. O <u>regardless the</u>   of
7. C
8. O   <u>aware the</u>   of
9. O   <u>attached bones</u>   to
10. I <u>to</u>
11. O <u>related the</u>   to
12. O <u>expert the</u>   on
13. C
14. I <u>by</u>
15. O <u>away the</u>   from
16. I <u>in</u>
17. I <u>of</u>
18. O <u>side the</u>   of
19. O <u>familiar people</u>   to
20. I <u>in</u>

Exercise 25.3

*1. Each
2. with a device
3. <u>in which</u> (which)
4. In
5. in the
6. <u>Many of</u> (Many)
7. Across
8. <u>in its</u> (on its)
*9. <u>live</u> (life)
10. with age
11. <u>during</u> (from)
12. with
13. <u>on</u> (in)

14. belongs one (belongs to one)
15. under the leadership of Samuel Gompers
16. are examples of
17. native of (native to)
18. There are some
19. on (in)
20. Since (For)
21. in use
22. thousands eggs (thousands of eggs)
23. In nowadays (Nowadays)
24. In (Since)
25. in width

Exercise 26.1

1. one   the water   fresh
2. The mineral   the most   fertilizers
3. The   a   electrical
4. Humor   American   the earliest   the present
5. The ozone   an   most   the Sun's
6. the early   a Cherokee   the   a North
7. The Goddard   New   the   the United   the eighteenth
8. Popcorn   the   corn
9. the most   research   the social   a well
10. the American   the   the twentieth   its   the   a hundred
11. The nineteenth   of   his
12. The Hawaiian   the most   the world

Exercise 26.2

1. The most (Most)
2. the (their)
3. an attention (attention)
4. a underwater (an underwater)
5. young (the young)
6. an only (the only)
7. the third (a third *or* one third)
8. the customers (their customers *or* customers)
9. imaginary (an imaginary)
10. the beef (beef)

11. the career (her career)
12. first (the first)
13. a honor (an honor)
14. a highest (the highest)
15. a human (the human)
*16. record (recording)
17. At beginning (At the beginning)
18. the history (history)
*19. open (opened)
*20. lose it (lose them)

Exercise 27.1

1. X chief source
2. X brightly colored
3. C
4. X is the Earth
5. X the Earth is
6. C
7. X miles longer
8. X they are
9. X natural habitats
10. X it possible
11. X dense enough
12. C
13. X almost entirely
14. C
15. X much too
16. X children's books
17. X Of all
18. X too much
19. X each second
20. X All of

Exercise 27.2

1. extremely interesting features of
2. barrier major (major barrier)
3. is light (light is)
4. The most famous form
5. enough large (large enough)
6. did anyone even attempt
7. a crop grown primarily
8. much more efficiently than
9. benefit both (both benefit)
10. that are embedded in it
11. were primary schools free
12. moving slow (slow moving)
13. in such diverse occupations as
14. is it (it is)

*15. <u>minerals grains</u> (mineral grains)

16. <u>original highly</u> (highly original)

17. Perhaps the greatest triumph

18. <u>one only</u> (only one)

19. <u>long feet</u> (feet long)

20. corporations hardly ever introduce

21. lies Maryland's Eastern Shore

22. <u>surrounded is</u> (is surrounded)

23. those that grow best

24. <u>satisfaction workers'</u> (workers' satisfaction)

25. <u>center trading</u> (trading center)

26. Of the four types of

*27. <u>lonely</u> (loneliness)

28. for even small boats to navigate

29. <u>none almost</u> (almost none)

30. is international trade today

Review Test F

Answer	**Explanation**
1. <u>on one time</u>	The wrong preposition is used; the phrase should correctly read *at one time*.
2. For her	Of the four choices, only a prepositional phrase correctly completes the sentence.
3. <u>a third</u>	Before an ordinal number (*third*), a definite article must be used: *the third*.
4. do redwood trees grow	After a negative adverb such as *rarely*, question word order must be used.
5. <u>on</u>	The preposition *in* is used before months.
6. <u>instead a</u>	The preposition *of* has been omitted from the phrase *instead of*.
7. are the most complex cells	Only this choice employs the correct word order.
8. <u>a enormous</u>	The article *an* must be used before words that begin with a vowel sound (*enormous*).
9. <u>themselves</u>	The correct pronoun is *them*. (The animals couldn't carry themselves!)
10. <u>psychology human</u>	The correct word order is *human psychology*.
11. a naturally occurring magnet	Only this choice uses the correct word order.
12. <u>railroads</u>	Only the second noun of a compound noun is pluralized: *railroad workers*.
13. <u>furnitures</u>	*Furniture* is an uncountable noun and cannot properly be pluralized.

Answer	Explanation
14. long been known as	Of the four choices, only this one uses the correct word order.
15. <u>itself</u>	The pronoun must be plural (*themselves*) to agree with its referent, *flying squirrels*.
16. <u>result of</u>	The verb *result* is used with the preposition *in*. (The noun *result* is followed by the preposition *of*.)
17. <u>all almost</u>	The correct word order is *almost all*.
18. <u>depend insects</u>	The preposition *on* must be used after the verb *depend*.
19. <u>enough safe</u>	The correct word order is adjective + *enough*: *safe enough*.
20. With its	A prepositional phrase is needed to complete this sentence.

Exercise 28

1. <u>both</u> (either)
2. or
3. but also
*4. <u>not longer</u> (no longer)
*5. <u>made</u>
*6. <u>it</u>
7. <u>and also</u> (but also)
8. and
9. <u>or</u> (nor)
10. <u>and</u> (or)
11. either
*12. <u>are used to</u> (used to)
*13. <u>produces</u> (produce)

14. so
15. <u>and</u> (but)
*16. <u>rust corrodes</u> (does rust corrode)
17. or
*18. <u>their</u> (its)
19. <u>as well as</u> (but also)
*20. not the only substance
*21. <u>require</u> (requires)
22. but when
23. <u>both frogs</u> (frogs)
24. both
25. but

Exercise 29

1. <u>like</u> (alike)
2. not as sweet as
3. <u>the most easiest</u> (the easiest)
4. <u>more strong</u> (stronger)
5. are larger than
6. <u>the more commonly</u> (the most commonly)
7. than trains do
8. <u>as</u> (than)
9. the higher its

10. Unlike
11. <u>worst</u> (worse)
12. <u>alike</u> (like)
13. saltier than
14. <u>like</u> (as)
15. more serious than
16. <u>more heavy</u> (heavier)
17. <u>bitter</u> (more bitter *or* bitterer)
18. as that of honeybees
19. <u>better known</u> (best known)
20. the same as
21. <u>less</u> (least)
*22. <u>contribution</u> (contributions)
23. <u>slender</u> (more slender *or* slenderer)
24. largest (larger)
25. differs from

Exercise 30

1. the Republican party
2. Peer group relations, the
3. the first
*4. which is a part of the Rocky Mountains,
5. The dancer
*6. The Internet is
7. a method
8. members of a strict religious sect,
9. the term
10. a
11. a tropical plant of the orchid family,
12. taste buds, groups of cells

Exercise 31

1. many New Englanders emigrated to the Midwest in the 1820s
2. pecans are the most important nut crop in the southern United States
3. Pluto was discovered by the astronomer Clyde Tombaugh in 1930
4. the accordion has played only a limited role in classical music
5. vultures do not have feathers on their heads and necks
6. Ansel Adams' photographs depicted the Western wilderness

7. a tangerine is easy to peel and its sections separate readily
8. state and local governments obtain most of their funds through taxation
9. Hawaii received its first European visitor in 1778, when Captain James Cook landed there
10. Robert Frost wrote poems that were
11. Cornell University was established in 1865 by Ezra Cornell
12. Kate Chopin wrote *Bayou Folk*, a book about the folklore of

Exercise 32

1. no
2. not
3. not (no)
4. not
5. without

6. none
*7. alike (like)
8. not
9. no (not)
10. no

11. No
12. without
13. Not (No)
14. never
15. no longer

Review Test G

Answer	Explanation
1. The Welland Ship Canal,	A noun phrase is needed to serve as subject of this sentence. (The phrase *one of Canada's . . .* is an appositive.)
2. most highest	The correct form of the superlative is *highest*.
3. and	The conjunction *but* is used before the word *rather* to show contrast.
4. almost as old as	The correct pattern is "*as* + adjective + *as . . .*"
5. and	The correct pattern is "whether A or B."
6. the farther away it was	This is a proportional statement; only this choice follows the pattern "The more A, the more B."
7. D. W. Griffith's epic film film *Birth of a Nation* was about the Civil War	The participial phrase *Released in* 1915 can logically modify only the title of a movie. For the first, second, and fourth choices, this is a misplaced modifier. Only in the third choice is the subject the title of a movie.
8. like	The correct pattern is "A and B are alike."
9. None of	The pronoun *none* means *not any* and is the only one of the choices that fits with the rest of the sentence. *No* and *Not* cannot be used before the article *the* and *Not one* must be used with *of*.
10. like	After certain verbs (including *serve*), the word *as* is used.
11. a	Of the four choices, only a noun phrase (an appositive) correctly completes the sentence.
12. no	Before a verb, the negative word *not* is needed.

Answer	Explanation
13. <u>and</u>	There is a contrast between the information in the two clauses, so the conjunction *but* should be used.
14. drugs can be used to treat the symptoms of many mental illnesses	The modifying phrase *Properly administered* can logically only go with the subject *drugs*. Used with any of the other subjects, this is a misplaced modifier.
15. <u>alike</u>	The correct pattern is "A looked like B."
16. <u>or</u>	After *neither*, the conjunction *nor* should be used.
17. A	Only an appositive (which precedes the subject) correctly completes this sentence.
18. <u>just like</u>	The phrase *just as* should be used before a clause.
19. No	Before a noun, the negative adjective *no* should be used.
20. <u>much rare</u>	The comparative *rarer* is required.
21. without	The negative word *without*—meaning *not having*—is the only one that fits in this sentence.
22. but	Because of the contrast between the two clauses, the conjunction *but* must be used.
23. either	The correct pattern is "either A or B."
24. <u>most closest</u>	The correct superlative form is *closest*.
25. Like	The correct pattern is, "Like A, B . . ."

Mini-Lessons for Section 2

Mini-Lesson 2.1

1. in (*or* with)
2. to
3. on
4. to
5. of   for

6. with
7. of
8. from
9. for
10. to

11. of
12. to (*or* for)
13. of
14. with   of
15. for

16. with
17. to
18. in
19. for
20. to

Mini-Lesson 2.2

1. to
2. to
3. into
4. for
5. for

6. at (*or* by)
7. to
8. for
9. to
10. of

11. to
12. with
13. to
14. of (*or* from)
15. to

Mini-Lesson 2.3

1. in of in of
2. of for
3. in of
4. on
5. with
6. of
7. of
8. of
9. to
10. to (*or* in)
11. of of
12. for for
13. of
14. on
15. of

Mini-Lesson 2.4

1. with
2. with
3. on
4. on
5. of
6. to to
7. in
8. with
9. with
10. in
11. with
12. with
13. to
14. on
15. to
16. for
17. in
18. for
19. in
20. to

Mini-Lesson 2.5

1. of
2. In of
3. with
4. to
5. in of
6. On of of
7. in to
8. to
9. of
10. by of
11. to
12. In of

Mini-Lesson 2.6

1. in
2. in
3. in in
4. in at
5. in (*or* at) at in
6. on in
7. in
8. in
9. on
10. in on on
11. in in
12. at on
13. in on
14. in
15. at on in (*or* of) in

Mini-Lesson 2.7

1. on in
2. at
3. at in
4. in
5. at
6. on
7. in, at
8. On
9. in
10. in
11. in in
12. at
13. in in
14. in
15. In
16. in
17. at
18. in
19. on
20. In on in

Mini-Lesson 2.8

1. with
2. by
3. for
4. by
5. without with
6. by
7. by
8. by in on
9. with
10. on in on in, by on
11. in at by to
12. for

Preview Test 3: Reading

1. The effects of an abundance of wood on the colonies
    The passage discusses the plentiful supply of wood in the colonies and the advantages and disadvantages this involved.

2. strikingly means *dramatically*.

3. they covered the entire continent.
    Paragraph 2 states, "The first colonists did not, as many people imagine, find an entire continent covered by a climax forest."

4. Plentiful means **abundant**.

5. was slightly higher than in previous years
    Paragraph 2 states, "By the end of the colonial era, the price of wood had risen slightly in eastern cities . . ."

6. They were usually built from materials other than wood.
    Paragraph 3 indicates that, in the colonies, ". . . buildings were made of wood to a degree unknown in Britain." Therefore, many British houses must have been made of materials other than wood.

7. To give an example of a product made from wood compounds
    According to paragraph 3, wood was the source of industrial compounds and charcoal is given as an example. Charcoal is a component of gunpowder.

8. The phrase follow suit means *do the same thing*.

9. It led to advances in technology.
    Paragraph 4 states that "Coke smelting led to technological innovations. . . ."

10. The opposite of cling to (which means *hold on to*) is **abandon**.

11. The X should go by paragraph 4.   *6 CH*

12. A family of artists
    The passage deals with the entire Peale family; the first and third choices are too specific, and the second is too general.

13. He refers to **Charles Willson Peale**.

14. Charles Willson Peale's painting was very lifelike
    The passage indicates that the portrait was "so realistic" that Washington mistook the painted figures for real ones.

15. The word displays is closest in meaning to *exhibits*.

16. The author defines the term *mastodon* in paragraph 2 as "a huge, extinct elephant." The other terms are undefined.

17. In what year was it founded?

    There is no information about when the museum was founded. All of the other questions are answered in the second paragraph: Charles Willson Peale found and prepared the animal exhibits; the museum was located in Philadelphia; its most popular exhibit, a mastodon's skeleton, was found on a farm in New York.

18. The word unearthed means *dug up*.

19. In this context, rage means *fashion*.

20. portraits of George Washington

    Charles Willson Peale painted over a dozen portraits of Washington (Paragraph 1); Rembrandt Peale also painted at least one (Paragraph 4).

21. His works show the same luminosity and attention to detail that the works of the Dutch masters show.

22. Sarah Miriam Peale

    Sarah Miriam Peale was Charles Willson Peale's niece (the daughter of his brother James Peale). Titian and Raphaelle are identified as Charles's sons in paragraph 1 and Reubens is identified as Charles's son in paragraph 3.

23. admiring

    The author praises the art and work of Charles Willson Peale and other members of the family; that, together with the absence of any critical comments, makes *admiring* the best choice.

24. The possibility of changing the Martian environment

    The main theme of this passage is the idea of transforming Mars.

25. The word stark is closest in meaning to *harsh*.

26. The word there refers to *Mars*.

27. carbon dioxide

    According to the passage, "The air there is 95% carbon dioxide."

28. Daytime temperatures may reach above freezing, but because the planet is blanketed by the mere wisp of an atmosphere, the heat radiates back into space.

29. Daytime temperatures are dangerously high.

    The passage states that "Daytime temperatures may reach above freezing," but there is no mention that temperatures ever become dangerously hot. The other characteristics are given in the first paragraph.

30. a possible means of warming Mars

    According to the passage, building up the atmosphere "could create a 'greenhouse effect' that would stop heat from radiating back into space." The author points out that it is the fact that heat radiates back into space that makes Mars so cold.

Section 3: Reading

31. The word thawed is closest in meaning to *melted*.

32. The word feasible is closest in meaning to *viable*.

33. could be started in 40 to 50 years

According to scientist Christopher McKay, the project could be started "in four or five decades"—forty or fifty years.

34. a knowledge of Earth's ecology

The passage indicates that the possibility of transforming Mars comes from a "more profound understanding of how Earth's ecology supports life."

35. The word they refers to *researchers*.

36. The word staggering means *astonishing*.   6CH

37. another factor that affects susceptibility to colds

The first paragraph indicates that age is "another" factor in susceptibility to colds; therefore, it is logical that a previous paragraph must deal with some other factor.

38. *Specific facts* is closest in meaning to the word particulars .

39. Its results apparently are relevant to the population as a whole.

Paragraph 1 states that the study "revealed particulars that seem to hold true for the general population."

40. Infant boys

Paragraph 1 indicates that "Infants are the most cold-ridden group" and that infant boys have more colds than infant girls.

41. The word incidence is closest in meaning to *rate*.

42. Children infect their parents with colds.

No matter what age they are, parents of young children show an increase in cold infections; it is reasonable to assume that these parents are infected by their children.

43. The phrase people in this age group refers to *people in their twenties*.

44. explain the relationship between income and frequency of colds

This paragraph deals with the influence of economics on incidence of colds.

45. The word cramped means *crowded*.

46. The study also found that economics plays an important role. ■ As income increases, the frequency at which colds are reported in the family decreases. ■ Families with the lowest income suffer a third more colds than families at the highest end. ■ Lower income generally forces people to live in more cramped quarters than those typically occupied by wealthier people, and crowded conditions increase the opportunities for the cold virus to travel from person to person. **Low income may also have an adverse effect on diet.** The degree to which deficient nutrition affects susceptibility to colds is not yet clearly established. ■ However, an inadequate diet is suspected of lowering resistance generally.

The sentence beginning "The degree . . ." involves nutrition. This connects with the missing sentence, which introduces the relationship between economics and diet.

47. The word $\boxed{\text{deficient}}$ is closest in meaning to **inadequate**.

48. neutral and objective

This is an objective, scientific report about factors that influence the rate at which people get colds.

49. what can be learned by growing roots in isolation

The passage generally discusses an experiment in which plant roots are grown in isolation.

50. The word $\boxed{\text{pronounced}}$ is closest in meaning to **obvious**.

51. (A)

52. The word $\boxed{\text{themselves}}$ is a reference to **roots**.

53. The scientists found that the nutrition of isolated roots is quite simple. ■ They require sugar (for carbon and an energy source), the usual minerals, and a few vitamins such as B_1 and niacin. **However, they do not require organic nitrogen compounds.** These roots can get along fine on mineral inorganic nitrogen. ■ Roots are capable of making their own proteins for new cell growth and other organic compounds such as nucleic acids. ■ As far as organic nitrogen compounds are concerned, then, roots can thrive without leaves. ■ All these activities by roots require energy, of course. ■ This comes from sugar. ■ The process of respiration in the cells of the root uses sugar to make the high energy compound ATP (adenosine triphosphate) which drives the biochemical reactions. ■ Respiration also requires oxygen, for the same reasons it does in all plants and animals.

The word *However* in the missing sentence indicates a contrast between that sentence and the previous sentence. The previous sentence tells what roots DO require for nutrition, The missing sentence tells what roots do NOT require—organic nitrogen. The following sentence says that the roots can do well with inorganic nitrogen.

54. The word $\boxed{\text{thrive}}$ means **get along fine**.

55. The word $\boxed{\text{this}}$ refers to **energy**.

56. an organic chemical

The passage says that through the process of respiration, the cells of the root use sugar to make the high energy compound ATP (adenosine triphosphate).

57. The word $\boxed{\text{intact}}$ means **whole**.

58. The phrase $\boxed{\text{come in handy}}$ means that the process is **useful**.

59. obtain organic compounds from the roots

The fact that roots provide organic nitrogen compounds is useful for "the growth of buds in the early spring when leaves are not yet functioning."

60. The findings of an experiment are explained.

The passage discusses an experiment involving plant roots and the significance of that experiment.

Exercise 33.1

1. (A) S		**3.** (A) X		**5.** (A) G		**7.** (A) G		**9.** (A) X	
(B) C		(B) S		(B) C		(B) C		(B) I	
(C) X		(C) C		(C) S		(C) X		(C) C	
2. (A) G		**4.** (A) X		**6.** (A) X		**8.** (A) C		**10.** (A) X	
(B) S		(B) C		(B) S		(B) X		(B) S	
(C) C		(C) I		(C) C		(C) I		(C) C	

Exercise 33.2

1. trace the development of American folk music

2. the special language of psychology

3. the contributions Gifford Pinchot made to American forestry

4. After initial success, off-Broadway theater began to decline.

5. the development of off-off-Broadway theater

6. There is considerable diversity in the size and the number of languages in language families of the Native Americans.

7. outline certain developments in mid-nineteenth century journalism

8. Other developments in journalism

9. objective

10. Earthquakes travel farther in the East than in the West.

11. Adults can utilize children's intense curiosity to help children learn more.

12. the function and history of settlement houses

13. admiration

14. The author first discusses Isadora Duncan's style of dance and then her life history.

15. They were unable to realize their goals, but they helped prepare the way for modern chemistry.

Exercise 33.3

1. the European pattern of rural settlement

2. the relative isolation of North American farm families

3. a contrast between a centripetal system of rural life and a centrifugal system

4. serve important functions in the body

5. it is important to eat the proper proportion of saturated fats and unsaturated fats.

6. excessive consumption of fats may be dangerous to one's health

7. The role of fats in human health

8. the process by which rocks are broken down

9. the evolution of soil

10. weathering breaks down rocks and leads to the development of soil

11. Peter Minuet's acquisition of Manhattan

12. the establishment of Fort Amsterdam

13. aspects of everyday life in New Amsterdam

14. A description of Peter Stuyvesant and his accomplishments

15. The fall of New Amsterdam

16. Forty years of Dutch rule in New Amsterdam

Exercise 34.1

1. Deer use their antlers chiefly to fight for mates or for leadership of a herd.

2. The velvety skin dries up and the deer rubs the skin off by scraping its antlers against trees.

3. On most deer, the first antlers are short and straight.

4. In spite of his failings, he did succeed in bringing the traditions of Native Americans to the attention of the American public.

5. Their aim was to achieve complete accuracy in creating a record of Native American life.

6. This coating had to resist salt corrosion as well as protect launch structures from hot rocket exhaust.

7. The first attempt lasted only twelve seconds and covered a distance of less than the wingspan of the largest airplanes of modern aircraft.

8. The dominant features of supermarkets are large in-store inventories on self-service aisles and centralized checkout lines.

9. It permits the supermarket, as well as other types of retail stores, to sell items that carry a higher margin than most food items.

10. By not offering delivery and by hiring cashiers and stockers rather than true sales personnel, supermarkets are able to keep prices at a relatively low level.

11. Since argon is extremely dense, there is less movement of the gas between the glass panes and therefore, less heat is lost.

12. When his family business failed, Irving was forced to become a full-time writer.

13. The wings of these three types of animals derive from different embryological structures but perform the same functions.

14. The pectoral fins of a fish, the wings of a bird, and the forelimbs of a mammal are all homologous structures.

Exercise 34.2

1. turkeys

2. is unknown today

3. 300 years

4. To settlements on ledges of canyon walls

5. sandstone

6. by means of ladders

7. food preparation

8. war

9. (paragraph 5)

10. The box zither.

11. Three or four

12. (A)

13. while sitting down

14. Helping to bring Appalachian dulcimers to the public's attention

15. Appalachian dulcimers are painstakingly fashioned by artisans in the mountains of West Virginia, Kentucky, Tennessee, and Virginia.

16. 1836

17. <u>In 1841 Dix accepted an invitation from the state legislature to teach classes at a prison in East Cambridge, Massachusetts.</u>

18. Massachusetts

19. obtain public lands

20. <u>Dix's success was due to her independent and thorough research, her gentle but persistent manner, and her ability to secure the help of powerful and wealthy supporters.</u>

21. are exposed to the surrounding water

22. a rebreather

23. 100 feet

24. breathe the same air again and again

25. plastic

26. <u>These divers get their air from a hose connected to compressors on a boat.</u>

27. a congressman

28. It had to be sold.

29. establishing new universities

30. Massachusetts

31. Farmers

32. To establish agricultural research stations

33. <u>Eventually they came to provide a full range of academic offerings, from anthropology to zoology.</u>

34. 69

35. (paragraph 1)

Exercise 35.1

1. B	5. A	9. C	13. B
2. C	6. A	10. A	14. C
3. C	7. A	11. B	15. C
4. C	8. C	12. A	

Exercise 35.2

1. They have more sophisticated nervous systems than was once thought.

2. may not be able to identify basic emotions through facial expressions

3. They showed the similarities between the mental organization of pigeons and that of humans.

4. agreement

5. less regularly

6. In the sunlight, the column of water may produce the colors of the rainbow.

7. A rise in the water level of a nearby river

8. the tubes of its plumbing system were much wider

9. have a more complex plumbing system

10. the geologists' original theory about Old Faithful was correct

11. shape

12. They reproduce efficiently.

13. don't know when tumbleweeds came to North America

14. are sources of popular information about tumbleweeds

15. was from southern Russia

16. found it difficult to classify the plant scientifically

17. aircraft did not need so much space to maneuver on the ground

18. an airport with only a few arrivals or departures

19. small terminals encircle the main terminal like satellites around a planet

20. the main terminal

21. the weather is bad

22. opposes the use of both sea walls and beach replenishment

23. These are communities in danger of beach erosion.

24. support his own position

Exercise 36.1

1. drab	7. course offerings	13. clear	19. afflict
2. garbage	8. stressed	14. hunted	20. terminate
3. carries	9. elective	15. fearful	21. cut
4. freight	10. group	16. advantages	22. minute
5. captures	11. haze	17. responsible	23. magnify
6. initiated	12. alone	18. disagreements	

Exercise 36.2

1. extremely rapid	24. Sturdy
2. Crucial	25. Shocks
3. The foundation was laid.	26. headed for
4. **recent immigrants**	27. **superbly**
5. land and buildings	28. **primitive**
6. supplemented	29. fastest
7. helpful	30. **emphasize**
8. **position**	31. Cooperative
9. predominated	32. name
10. allowed to do as it pleased	33. tormenting
11. **competed**	34. Criticism
12. fiercely	35. Dangerous
13. **unique to**	36. enemies
14. classify	37. **ordered**
15. Ornamental	38. control
16. **broad**	39. provides new information about
17. observe	40. unstoppable
18. Variety	41. **Altering**
19. **startling**	42. **more slowly**
20. not nearly	43. complicated
21. basic	44. Hints
22. peaceful	45. previously
23. represent	

Exercise 37.1

1. <u>paintings</u>
2. <u>The anemone</u>
   <u>its nest</u>
3. flowers
4. <u>a flat kite</u>
   <u>tail</u>
5. <u>Water</u>
6. strands
7. <u>smaller pieces</u>
8. <u>Leaves</u>
9. New York City
10. <u>mushrooms and other fungi</u>
11. <u>Hamlin Garland</u>
    <u>William Dean Howells</u>
12. <u>The strange formations</u>
13. viruses
14. <u>satellite photography</u>
15. <u>An elephant</u>

Exercise 37.2

1. **the pieces**
2. **trucks**
3. surface mining
4. **Water**
5. **The metal particles**
6. mineral concentration
7. **the ore particles**
8. **The mountain's summit**
9. **glaciers**
10. alpine meadows
11. **The Wonderland Trail**
12. **Their tracks**
13. migratory mammal
14. **The males**
15. The Pribilof Islands
16. **tiny plants and animals**
17. **Designers**
18. **importance**
19. **A circle and an oval**
20. **a triangle**
21. unity
22. **illustrations**
23. picture books
24. three- or four-year olds

Exercise 38

1. When a mammal is young, it looks much like a smaller form of an adult. ■ However, animals that undergo metamorphosis develop quite differently from mammals. ■ The young of these animals, which are called larvae, look very little like the mature forms and have a very different way of life. ■ Take the example of butterflies and caterpillars, which are the larval form of butterflies. ■ **Butterflies have two pairs of wings and six legs and feed on the nectar of flowers.** ■ Caterpillars, on the other hand, are wingless and have more than six legs. They move by crawling and feed on leaves. ■ To become adults, the larvae must radically change their forms.

2. To accomplish this change, a larva must go through the process of metamorphosis. ■ It does this in the second stage of life, called the pupa stage. ■ When they are ready to pupate, caterpillars settle in sheltered positions. ■ Some spin a cocoon around themselves. ■ The caterpillar then sheds its old skin and grows a protective pupal skin. ■ Inside this skin, the body of the caterpillar gradually transforms itself. ■ The wingbuds, which were under the caterpillar's skin, grow into wings. ■ When the change is complete the pupal skin splits open and the butterfly emerges. ■ **At first it is damp and its wings are curled up.** ■ But soon it dries out, its wings unfurl, and it flies off. ■ Now it is ready to mate and to lay eggs that will develop into larvae.

3. The process of miniaturization began in earnest with the transistor, which was invented in 1947. ■ It was much smaller than the smallest vacuum tube it was meant to replace and not needing a filament, it consumed far less power and generated virtually no waste heat. ■ There was almost no limit to how small the transistor could be once engineers had learned how to etch electronic circuits onto a substrate of silicon. ■ In the 1950s the standard radio had five vacuum tubes and dozens of resistors and capacitors, all hand-wired and soldered onto a chassis about the size of a hardbound book. ■ **Today all that circuitry and much more can fit into a microprocessor smaller than a postage stamp.** ■ In fact, the limiting factor in making appliances smaller is not the size of the electronic components but the human interface. ■ There is no point in reducing the size of a palm-held computer much further unless humans can evolve smaller fingers.

4. It is believed that the first Americans were hunters who arrived by way of the only link between the hemispheres, the Siberian-Alaskan land bridge. ■ This strip of land remained above water until about 10,000 years ago. **More recent arrivals no doubt took the same route, crossing on winter ice.** ■ These migrants unquestionably brought with them the skills to make weapons, fur clothing, and shelters against the bitter cold. ■ It seems safe to assume that they also brought myths and folktales from the Old World. ■ But which myths and which folktales?

5. Among myths, the most impressive candidate for Old World origin is the story of the Earth Diver. ■ This is the story of a group of water creatures who take turns diving for a piece of solid land. ■ The duck, the muskrat, the turtle, the crawfish, or some other animal succeeds but has to dive so deep that by the time it returns to the surface, it is half-drowned or dead. **But in its claws, the other animals find a bit of mud.** ■ The animals magically enlarge this tiny piece of solid land until it becomes the Earth. ■ Not every Native American tribe has a myth about the creation of the world, but of those that do, the Earth Diver myth is the most common. ■ It is found in all regions of North America except the Southwestern United States and the Arctic regions, and is also found in many locations in Asia and the Pacific Islands.

6. Another common myth is that of the Theft of Fire. ■ In this story, a creature sets out to steal fire from a distant source, obtains it, often through trickery, and carries it home. ■ The best known version of this story is the Greek myth of Prometheus. ■ Other Old World versions of this story are told in Central Asia, India, and Africa. **In the New World, it appears among many Native American tribes west of the Rocky Mountains and in the American Southeast.** ■ In some New World locations it is replaced by Theft of the Sun, Theft of Daylight, or Theft of Heat stories.

7. When drawing human figures, children often make the head too large for the rest of the body. ■ A recent study offers some insight into this common disproportion in children's illustrations. ■ As part of the study, researchers asked children between four and seven years old to make several drawings of adults. ■ When they drew frontal views of these subjects, the size of the heads was markedly enlarged. **However, when the children drew rear views of the adults, the size of the heads was not nearly so exaggerated.** The researchers suggest that children draw bigger heads when they know they must leave room for facial details. ■ Therefore, the distorted head size in children's illustrations is a form of planning ahead and not an indication of a poor sense of scale.

8. It has been observed that periods of maximum rainfall occur in both the northern and southern hemispheres at about the same time. ■ This phenomenon cannot be adequately explained on a climatological basis, but meteors may offer a plausible explanation. ■ When the Earth encounters a swarm of meteors, each meteor striking the upper reaches of the atmosphere is vaporized by frictional heat. ■ The resulting debris is a fine smoke or powder. ■ This "stardust" then floats down into the lower atmosphere, where such dust might readily serve as nuclei upon which ice crystals or raindrops could form. **Confirmation that this phenomenon actually happens is found in the observed fact that increases in world rainfall come about a month after meteor systems are encountered in space.** ■ The delay of a month allows time for the dust to fall through the upper atmosphere. ■ Occasionally, large meteors leave visible traces of dust. ■ In a few witnessed cases, dust has remained visible for over an hour. ■ In one extreme instance—the great meteor that broke up in the sky over Siberia in 1908—the dust cloud traveled all over the world before disappearing.

9. Lawn tennis is a comparatively modern modification of the ancient game of court tennis. ■ Major Walter C. Wingfield thought that something like court tennis might be played outdoors on the grass and in 1873 he introduced his new game under the name *Sphairistikè* at a lawn party in Wales. **It was an immediate success and spread rapidly, but the original name quickly disappeared.** ■ Players and spectators soon began to call the new game "lawn tennis." ■ In 1874 a woman named Mary Outerbridge returned to New York with the basic equipment of the game, which she had obtained from a British Army store in Bermuda. ■ The first game of lawn tennis in the United States was played on the grounds of the Staten Island Cricket and Baseball Club in 1874.

10. The game went on in a haphazard fashion for a number of years. **Then in 1879, standard equipment, rules, and measurements for the court were instituted.** A year later, the U.S. Lawn Tennis Association was formed. ■ International matches for the Davis Cup began in 1900. ■ They were played at Chestnut Hill, Massachusetts between British and American players. ■ The home team won this first championship match.

11. Photosynthesis is the process by which plants capture the Sun's energy to convert water and carbon dioxide into sugars to fuel their growth. **This process cannot take place without chlorophyll.** ■ In fact, chlorophyll is so essential to the life of plants that it forms almost

instantly in seedlings as they come in contact with sunlight. ■ A green pigment, chlorophyll is responsible for the green coloring of plants. ■ But what turns the leaves of deciduous plants brilliant red and orange and gold in the autumn?

12. Trees do not manufacture new pigments for fall. ■ Orange, red, yellow, and other colored pigments are present in the leaves throughout the spring and summer. ■ However, these are masked by the far greater quantity of chlorophyll. ■ When the days grow shorter and temperatures fall, trees sense the onset of fall. ■ They form an "abscission layer." ■ This layer is a barrier of tissue at the base of each leaf stalk. **It prevents nourishment from reaching the leaf and, conversely, prevents sugar created in the leaf from reaching the rest of the tree.** ■ Thus, sugar builds up in the leaf, causing the chlorophyll to break down. ■ The greens of summer then begin to fade. ■ The orange, red, yellow, and brown pigments now predominate, giving the leaves their vibrant autumn colors.

13. Prairie dogs are among the most sociable wild animals of North America. ■ They are members of the squirrel family. ■ Why they are called "dogs" is a mystery. **They bear no resemblance to dogs, except that their call sounds a little like the bark of a small dog.** ■ At one time, they thrived nearly everywhere on the semi-arid prairie lands of the Great Plains. ■ Native Americans even used prairie dog colonies as landmarks on the relatively featureless plains. ■ Today, though, their range is greatly reduced. ■ They survive in large numbers mainly in protected areas such as Devil's Tower National Monument, Wind Cave National Park, and Theodore Roosevelt National Park.

14. Prairie dogs live in densely populated areas called towns. ■ Large towns are divided into wards which are separated by topographic features such as hills, roads, streams, or belts of trees. ■ Wards, in turn, are divided into coteries. ■ The typical coterie contains one adult male, three to four adult females, and several juveniles. **However, coterie size can vary anywhere from two to about forty individuals.** ■ If two or more adult males reside in the same coterie, one is dominant. ■ The residents of each coterie protect their territory from invaders, including prairie dogs from other coteries.

15. In the early nineteenth century, the United States was still an overwhelmingly rural nation. ■ Shrewd showmen saw that there was a fortune to be made in taking shows to the people. ■ By 1820 there were some 30 small "mud show" circuses (so named because of the treacherous muddy roads and fields over which their wagons had to travel). **The number of shows increased rapidly after the first "Big Top" circus tent was introduced in 1826.** ■ This innovation enabled circuses to perform in rain or shine. ■ Like circuses today, early nineteenth century circuses featured wild animal acts, bareback riders, acrobats, trapeze and high wire artists, circus bands, and, of course, clowns. ■ It was not until after the Civil War, however, that circuses became huge, three-ring spectacles involving hundreds of performers.

Review Test H

1. Advantages of biological agents over chemical ones
The passage generally concerns the advantages of biological agents and the disadvantages of chemical agents.

2. The word marring means *spoiling*.

3. The word | hamper | is closest in meaning to the word *impede*.

4. Weeds

   The author defines *weeds* as "any plants that thrive where they are unwanted" (sentence 2). No definitions are offered for the other terms.

5. The word | harm | is closest in meaning to *injure*.

6. It is occasionally required.

   Paragraph 2 says herbicides are sometimes necessary.

7. They are more easily available.

   The first choice is given in paragraph 4, which says that biological agents "leave crops and other plants untouched." The second choice is also given; chemical agents "harm workers who apply them." The fourth choice is given in paragraph 4; "biological agents can be administered only once" while chemical agents "typically must be used several times per growing season."

8. insects and microorganisms

   According to the passage, the living organisms used to kill weeds are "primarily insects and microorganisms."

9. The biological agents now used to control weeds are environmentally benign and offer the benefit of specificity. ■ They can be chosen for their ability to attack selected targets and leave crops and other plants untouched, including plants that might be related to the target weeds. **In contrast, some of the most effective chemicals kill virtually all the plants they come in contact with.** ■ They spare only those that are naturally resistant or those that have been genetically modified for resistance. ■ Furthermore, a number of biological agents can be administered only once, after which no added applications are needed. ■ Chemicals typically must be used several times per growing season.

   The phrase *In contrast* indicates that the missing sentence must follow a sentence that expresses an opposite idea. The main point of the missing sentence is that chemicals kill all the plants they come in contact with. The previous sentence talks about how biological agents are selective in the plants they kill.

10. In this context, | applications | means *treatments* (with biological agents).

11. The word | they | refers to *biological approaches*.

12. The word | standard | is closest in meaning to *conventional*.

13. A problem is described and possible solutions are compared.

    The problem is the need to control weeds; the possible solutions are the use of chemical or biological agents.

14. favorable

    The author refers to the fact that Bernstein's score is "brilliant," that Stephen Sondheim "revealed a remarkable talent," and that Jerome Robbins' choreography is "electrifying." All of these positive factors, and the absence of negative ones, add up to a favorable attitude.

15. In the early 1950s.

    Paragraph 1 says the play "is set in the early 1950s."

16. were families in Shakespeare's play

Paragraph 1 mentions "The Montagues and Capulets of Shakespeare's play" and compares them with the Jets and Sharks in *West Side Story*.

17. The word   rival   means *opposing*.

18. The plot tells the story of Maria, a Puerto Rican whose brother Bernardo is the leader of the Sharks, and of Tony, a member of the Jets.

19. Stephen Sondheim

Paragraph 2 states: "Stephen Sondheim . . . revealed a remarkable talent for writing lyrics."

20. A   score   is the written form of a piece of music.

21. The word   electrifying   is closest in meaning to *thrilling*.

22. The word   ones   refers to *Academy Awards*.

23. Dance was not such an important feature in them.

The second paragraph says that "Before *West Side Story*, no one thought that dance could be as integral to a narrative as the music and the lyrics. But the dances in *West Side Story* are among the most thrilling elements of the play."

24. 734

Paragraph 3 indicates that, after it first opened, the play ran for 734 performances in New York.

25. a formal social occasion

Paragraph 1 states that "the black tie [i.e., very formal] audience treated the occasion . . . as a social affair."

26. Karl Benz

Paragraph 2 states that "German engineer Karl Benz built what are regarded as the first modern cars in the mid-1880s."

27. But the United States pioneered the merchandising of the automobile.

28. 8,000

There were about 8,000 people at the 1900 National Automobile Show, according to paragraph 1. By coincidence, this was the same number of automobiles as there were in the United States in 1900 (paragraph 3).

29.   By happenstance   means *Coincidentally*.

30. 1,000

According to the passage, only around 4,000 cars were assembled in the United States in 1900, and only a quarter of those were gasoline powered (paragraph 3). One quarter of 4,000 is 1,000.

31. electricity

Paragraph 4 states that "the show's audience favored electric cars because they were quiet."

32. The word   fragrant   is most nearly opposite in meaning to the word *smelly*.

33. hide strong smells

According to the passage, "The Duryea Motor Wagon Company . . . offered a fragrant additive designed to mask the smells of the naphtha that it burned."

34. The word │cumbersome│ is closest in meaning to *clumsy*.

35. a Duryea

Paragraph 4 indicates that the Gasmobile, Franklin, and Orient steered with tillers (devices used to steer boats); the Duryea probably used a steering wheel.

36. The word │well-to-do│ is closest in meaning to **wealthy**.

37. These early model cars were practically handmade and were not very dependable. ■ They were basically toys of the well-to-do. ■ In fact, Woodrow Wilson, then a professor at Princeton University and later President of the United States, predicted that automobiles would cause conflict between the wealthy and the poor. ■ However, among the exhibitors at the 1900 show was a young engineer named Henry Ford. **The cars he exhibited at the 1900 show apparently attracted no special notice.** ■ But before the end of the decade, he would revolutionize the automobile industry with his Model T Ford. ■ The Model T, first produced in 1909, featured a standardized design and a streamlined method of production. ■ Its lower costs made it available to the mass market.

The missing sentence clearly refers to the exhibitor, Henry Ford. The first word in the following sentence is *but*, indicating contrast. The contrast involves the fact that, at the 1900 show, Ford's cars were not especially noticed, but in a few years, he would completely change the industry.

38. $1,500

Paragraph 6 indicates that the highest-priced cars at the show sold for $1,500 in 1900 dollars.

39. give the highlights of Georgia O'Keeffe's artistic career

The first choice is not correct; the author is not critical of O'Keeffe's style. The second choice is too specific. There is no comparison of abstract art and landscape art, so the third choice is not correct. The fourth choice is the best statement of the author's purpose.

40. Chicago and New York City

According to the first paragraph, O'Keefe studied at the Art Institute of Chicago (1905) and the Art Students League in New York City (1907–1908).

41. The word │frequented│ is closest in meaning to *visited*.

42. Georgia O'Keeffe was born in Sun Prairie, Wisconsin in 1887. ■ She studied at the Art Institute of Chicago (1905) and the Art Students League in New York City (1907-1908). ■ Beginning as an advertising illustrator, she supported herself until 1918 by teaching art in public schools and colleges in Texas. **After that date, she devoted herself entirely to painting.** ■ Her paintings were first exhibited in 1919 at "291," an experimental art gallery in New York City owned by the photographer Alfred Stieglitz, which was frequented by some of the most influential artists of the time. ■ O'Keeffe married Stieglitz in 1924.

The phrase *that date* in the missing sentence refers to the year 1918, and is a link to the previous sentence. Also, the previous sentence is about O'Keeffe's teaching career and the following sentence about her career as a painter, while the missing sentence is about her dedicating the rest of her life to painting.

43. The word enigmatic is closest in meaning to *mysterious*.

44. C

According to the passage, she "most often painted desert landscapes" after a trip to New Mexico in 1929.

45. A trip to the Southwest

Paragraph 3 indicates that her "style changed dramatically . . . during a visit to New Mexico." The reference to the "Southwestern sun" tells you that New Mexico is in the Southwest.

46. The word blanched is closest in meaning to *whitened*.

47. The word hues is closest in meaning to *colors*.

48. The word they refers to *paintings*.

49. 1947

Her husband died in 1946; she moved permanently to New York the following year—1947.

50. continued to be successful

Paragraph 4 states that she became "the dean of Southwestern painters and one of the best known of American artists." There is no information to support the other choices.

Mini-Lessons for Section 3: Vocabulary Building

Mini-Lesson 3.1

1. (A)	**4.** (A)	**7.** (A)	**10.** (C)	**13.** (B)
2. (C)	**5.** (B)	**8.** (B)	**11.** (A)	**14.** (A)
3. (A)	**6.** (B)	**9.** (C)	**12.** (B)	**15.** (C)

Mini-Lesson 3.2

1. (C)	**4.** (C)	**7.** (A)	**10.** (A)	**13.** (C)
2. (C)	**5.** (B)	**8.** (B)	**11.** (B)	**14.** (C)
3. (A)	**6.** (B)	**9.** (C)	**12.** (C)	

Mini-Lesson 3.3

1. (C)	**4.** (B)	**7.** (A)	**10.** (B)	**13.** (A)
2. (A)	**5.** (B)	**8.** (C)	**11.** (A)	**14.** (A)
3. (B)	**6.** (C)	**9.** (A)	**12.** (C)	

Mini-Lesson 3.4

1. (C)	**3.** (A)	**5.** (C)	**7.** (A)	**9.** (B)	**11** (B)
2. (C)	**4.** (B)	**6.** (B)	**8.** (C)	**10.** (B)	

Mini-Lesson 3.5

1. (A)	**4.** (A)	**7.** (A)	**10.** (A)	**13.** (A)	**16.** (B)
2. (A)	**5.** (B)	**8.** (B)	**11.** (C)	**14.** (C)	**17.** (B)
3. (B)	**6.** (C)	**9.** (C)	**12.** (B)	**15.** (A)	

Mini-Lesson 3.6

1. (B)	**4.** (B)	**7.** (C)	**10.** (C)	**13.** (A)	**16.** (A)
2. (B)	**5.** (A)	**8.** (C)	**11.** (C)	**14.** (C)	
3. (C)	**6.** (C)	**9.** (A)	**12.** (B)	**15.** (C)	

Mini-Lesson 3.7

1. (C)	**4.** (A)	**7.** (A)	**10.** (A)	**13.** (B)
2. (B)	**5.** (A)	**8.** (B)	**11.** (C)	**14.** (B)
3. (B)	**6.** (C)	**9.** (C)	**12.** (B)	

Mini-Lesson 3.8

1. (C)	**4.** (C)	**7.** (B)	**10.** (B)	**13.** (A)	**16.** (B)
2. (C)	**5.** (C)	**8.** (C)	**11.** (A)	**14.** (C)	**17.** (C)
3. (A)	**6.** (A)	**9.** (C)	**12.** (B)	**15.** (C)	

Mini-Lesson 3.9

1. (C)	**3.** (C)	**5.** (B)	**7.** (B)	**9.** (B)	**11.** (A)
2. (C)	**4.** (A)	**6.** (B)	**8.** (A)	**10.** (A)	

Mini-Lesson 3.10

1. (A)	**4.** (B)	**7.** (C)	**10.** (C)
2. (B)	**5.** (B)	**8.** (A)	**11.** (B)
3. (C)	**6.** (C)	**9.** (B)	**12.** (C)

Mini-Lesson 3.11

1. (C)	**4.** (A)	**7.** (B)	**10.** (B)	**13.** (B)	**16.** (A)
2. (B)	**5.** (C)	**8.** (A)	**11.** (C)	**14.** (C)	
3. (B)	**6.** (C)	**9.** (A)	**12.** (B)	**15.** (B)	

Mini-Lesson 3.12

1. (A)	**4.** (C)	**7.** (A)	**10.** (A)	**13.** (A)
2. (A)	**5.** (B)	**8.** (C)	**11.** (C)	**14.** (B)
3. (C)	**6.** (C)	**9.** (C)	**12.** (B)	**15.** (A)

Mini-Lesson 3.13

1. (A)	4. (B)	7. (B)	10. (A)	13. (B)
2. (C)	5. (C)	8. (A)	11. (C)	14. (C)
3. (B)	6. (C)	9. (B)	12. (B)	

Mini-Lesson 3.14

1. (B)	4. (B)	7. (C)	10. (B)	13. (B)	16. (B)
2. (B)	5. (C)	8. (C)	11. (B)	14. (C)	17. (C)
3. (C)	6. (B)	9. (B)	12. (A)	15. (A)	18. (B)

Mini-Lesson 3.15

1. (C)	4. (C)	7. (B)	10. (A)	13. (B)
2. (A)	5. (C)	8. (C)	11. (A)	14. (B)
3. (C)	6. (A)	9. (B)	12. (A)	

Mini-Lesson 3.16

1. (C)	4. (A)	7. (A)	10. (A)	13. (C)	16. (C)
2. (B)	5. (A)	8. (B)	11. (B)	14. (C)	
3. (A)	6. (C)	9. (C)	12. (A)	15. (A)	

Mini-Lesson 3.17

1. (C)	3. (C)	5. (C)	7. (C)	9. (A)	11. (B)
2. (B)	4. (A)	6. (A)	8. (B)	10. (C)	12. (A)

Exercise 39.1

Answers will vary. These analyses are given as samples.

Type A

Prompt 1

This prompt says that there are two opinions regarding basic educational philosophy. Education can emphasize either competition or cooperation. I have to decide which of these I want to support.

If I choose to support cooperation, I need to show how learning to cooperate will be useful in later life—for example, being able to work with one's colleagues. If I choose to defend the opposite idea, I can show the advantages of being a competitive person—in sports, in business, and so on. Or I might say that a good education should teach people that at times they must cooperate well and at times they must be strong competitors.

Prompt 2

When writing this essay, I have to show the benefits of either on-campus living or off-campus living. One advantages of dorm living is convenience. Another is that it provides opportunities for making friends. I could support this by giving examples of how dorm living makes life easy for students and encourages them to interact with other students. The main advantages of off-campus living are independence and privacy, I suppose. If I choose to take this side, I'll need to think of ways that living off-campus can make someone a better student and better prepared for adult life.

Type B

Prompt 3

There are two possible approaches to writing this essay. I can give a number of reasons why athletes and entertainers make far too much money for what they do, especially when compared with people who contribute much more to society than they do. If I choose to defend the other point of view, I have to justify these large salaries. I could say that, like any other workers, they are simply getting the salary that people are willing to give them for their services, and also that they bring a lot of entertainment and enjoyment to people.

Prompt 4

I could choose to agree with this statement. If I do, I have to show how taking a wide variety of classes makes a person well-rounded and better informed. I might say that it is fine for graduate students to specialize, but that undergraduates need to be generalists with some knowledge of history, science, math, art, and all the other important fields. On the other hand, if I take the opposite side, I have to give reasons why it is a good idea to concentrate only on one field of interest. I might say, for example, that for students in scientific and technical fields, there is so much to learn in four years that it is impossible for them to take many electives.

Type C
Prompt 5

For this prompt I must choose a figure from the past that I want to talk to. It could be someone internationally famous, such as Julius Caesar, Simon Bolívar, Abraham Lincoln, or Mahatma Gandhi. Or I could choose to speak to someone who is important to me personally, such as my great-great-grandfather. It will probably be best if I choose someone I know quite a bit about, and preferably someone in a field that I am interested in. I could choose Pele, for example, because I'm interested in football, or Adam Smith because I'm interested in economics. The most important thing is to have good reasons why I want to talk to the person that I choose, and to have some specific questions I'd like to ask this person.

Prompt 6

The prompt says that I can fund any one of a variety of city services. To write this essay, I need to decide what kind of service my hometown needs most. For example, if there is a high crime rate, then I could make a good case for funding the police department. It would probably be easy to explain why funding should go to schools or hospitals, because almost any community needs improvements in education and health care.

Exercise 39.2

Answers will vary.

Exercise 39.3

Answers will vary.

Exercise 40.1

Answers will vary.

Exercise 40.2

Answers will vary.

Exercise 40.3

Answers will vary.

Exercise 41.1

There may be several ways to join some of these sentences.

1. One of the most important holidays in my country is Independence Day, **which** is celebrated on September 16th.

2. Young children have a special talent for language learning, **so** they should be taught other languages at an early age.
    Because young children have a special talent for language learning, they should be taught other languages at an early age.

3. **Since** my brother began studying at the university, he has taken several large classes.

4. **Although / Even though** some forms of advertising serve a useful purpose, many other forms do not.
    Some forms of advertising serve a useful purpose, **but** many other forms do not.

5. A friend is an acquaintance **who** will help you whenever possible.

6. I believe corporations should do more to recycle materials **and** to reduce air pollution.

7. Small classes are the best environment for learning, **but** sometimes universities must have large classes.
    Even though / Although small classes are the best environment for learning, sometimes universities must have large classes.

8. We must develop alternative sources of energy, **or** air pollution will get worse and worse.

Exercise 41.2

Answers will vary for sentences 1–4.

5. In small classes, students get more personal attention.

6. If I needed to get in touch with a business associate, I would use e-mail.

7. Again and again, I have asked myself that question.

8. Because of its long and fascinating history, my favorite place in the world to visit is Greece.

Exercise 41.3

(Introduction 2)

Many students believe that small classes offer much better educational opportunities than large ones. **However**, in my experience, that is not necessarily true. I believe that, with a good teacher, a large class can provide as good a learning opportunity as a small one.

(Body 1)

However, other people believe that space research has provided many benefits to humankind. They point out that hundreds of useful products, from personal computers to heart pacemakers to freeze-dried foods, are the direct or indirect results of space research. They say that weather and communication satellites, which are also products of space research, have benefitted people all over the globe. In addition to these practical benefits, supporters of the space program point to the scientific knowledge that has been acquired about the Sun, the Moon, the planets, and even our own Earth as a result of space research.

(Body 2)

When I was an undergraduate student, most of the large classes I took were introductory classes for first- and second- year students. For example, I took classes in world history and economics that had over 100 students and met in large lecture halls. I think these classes were as good as some of the small classes I took later. At the basic level, the lectures that a professor gives are basically the same no matter what size the class is. **Moreover**, the professors who taught these classes seemed more enthusiastic and energetic than the teachers I had in smaller classes. **Personally,** I think they enjoyed having a large audience!

One supposed advantage of small classes is that there is usually a lot more interaction among students and between the teacher and the students than in large ones. **However**, in the large classes I took, there were discussion sessions held every week with a graduate teaching assistant in which there was a lot of interaction. **Besides**, the teachers for these classes had long office hours, and they were always willing to answer questions and talk over problems.

(Body 3)

The most obviously important characteristic of jet travel is the high speed involved. A hundred years ago, it took weeks to cross the Atlantic or Pacific oceans by ship. **However**, today, those same trips can be completed in a matter of hours. One can attend a meeting in Paris and have dinner in New York the same day. These amazing speeds have changed people's concepts of space. Today the world is much smaller than it was in the past.

Another important aspect of jet travel is its relatively low cost. An international journey one hundred years ago was extremely expensive. Only wealthy people could afford to travel comfortably, in first class. Poor people had to save for years to purchase a ticket, and the conditions in which they traveled were often miserable. Today it is possible for more and more people in every country to travel in comfort. **Thus** it is possible for business people to do business all over the world, for students to attend universities in other countries, and for tourists to take vacations anywhere in the world.

(Conclusion 1)

I agree with those people who support space research and want it to continue. Space research, as shown, has already brought many benefits to humanity. Perhaps it will bring even more benefits in the future, ones that we can't even imagine now. **Moreover**, just as individual people need challenges to make their lives more interesting, I believe the human race itself needs a challenge, and I think that the peaceful exploration of outer space provides just such a challenge.

(Conclusion 2)

In conclusion, I don't think that the size of class is very important. I think that learning depends more on the quality of the teaching than on the number of students in the class.

(Conclusion 3)

To summarize, the speed and low cost of international jet travel have changed the world. Individual nations are not as isolated as they were in the past, and people now think of the whole planet as they once thought of their own hometowns.

Exercise 41.4

1. I believe that women should have the right to serve in the military. **However**, I don't believe that they should be assigned to combat roles.

2. Many actors, rock musicians, and sports stars receive huge amounts of money for the work that they do. **For example**, a baseball player was recently offered a contract worth over twelve million dollars. **Personally**, I feel that this is far too much to pay a person who simply provides entertainment.

3. The development of the automobile has had a great impact on people everywhere. **Likewise**, the development of high-speed trains has had an impact on people in many countries, including my home country of France.

4. I used to work in a restaurant when I was in college. I realize what a difficult job restaurant work is. **Therefore**, whenever I go out to eat, I try to leave a good tip for my waiter or waitress.

5. Many people would agree with the idea that the best use for the open space in our community is to build a shopping center in this community. **On the other hand**, there are other people who feel we should turn this open space into a park.

6. The use of computer technology has had a major impact on the way many people work. **Furthermore**, it has also changed the way many people spend their leisure time.

Exercise 41.5

There are a number of ways to correctly rewrite this essay.

There are certain people who always like to take their vacations in the same place. They return from a vacation and ask themselves, "When can I go back there again?" There are other people who like to go many places. They like to do many different things on their vacations. When they return from a vacation, they ask themselves, "Where can I go next?"

My parents are perfect examples of the first kind of people. They always like to go to a lake in the mountains where they went on their honeymoon. They bought a vacation cabin there several years after they were married. They have gone there two or three times a year for over twenty-five years. My parents have made friends with the people who also own cabins there. They enjoy getting together with them. Both my parents enjoy sailing and swimming and my father likes to go fishing. My parents enjoy variety, but they say they can get variety by going to their cabin at different times of the year. They particularly like to go there in the autumn when the leaves are beautiful.

I am an example of a person who likes to go to different places for her vacation. When I was a child, I went to my parents' cabin, but when I got older, I wanted to travel to many different places. I spent a lot of time and money learning how to ski, so I wanted to travel to places where I could ski, such as Switzerland. I was interested in visiting historic places, so I went to Angkor Wat in Cambodia even though it was difficult to get there. I would like to go to Egypt because I want to see the pyramids and to Rome to see the Coliseum.

Although I enjoy going to familiar places, I find that going to strange places is more exciting. The world is so huge and exciting that I don't want to go to the same place twice. Still, I understand my parents' point of view. They believe that you can never get to know a place too well.

Exercise 41.6

Answers will vary.

Exercise 42.1

There are several ways in which some of the errors in these paragraphs can be corrected.

Paragraph 1

There ~~is~~ *are* many species of animals in the world threatened with extinction. One threatened animal is *the*∧ tiger. I believe that ∧*it* is very important that governments protect ∧*the* tiger. In Indonesia tigers ∧*are* protected by the government. ∧*Still* many of them ~~is~~ *are* killed every year.

Paragraph 2

~~The~~ *T*echnology has ∧*a* had major impact in many ~~field~~ *fields*. Nowadays we can't even ~~suppose~~ *imagine* business, communication, or ~~travelling~~ *travel* without computers. I want to discuss ~~about~~ the impact of computers on ~~the~~ education. ~~The~~ *M*odern technology has made ~~live easy~~ *life easier* for students and professors. If a student ~~want~~ *wants* to contact ~~with~~ a professor, ~~you haven't problem.~~ *it's simple.* ~~It is enough~~ *The student* ~~only to send professor's an e-mail and you haven't to go to~~ *can send the professor an e-mail rather than go to his or her* office. ~~More over~~ *Moreover,* many ~~university~~ *universities have* created special ~~network~~ *networks* for students in order to make the ~~studying~~ process ∧*of studying* easy for ~~its~~ *them.* ~~students. For such kind net you could enter only~~ *Students may enter this kind of network* by using ~~your~~ *their* ∧~~pass word~~ *passwords* and identification number. There are many categories

a student
~~you~~ ∧ can chose to enter, such as "student tools" or "assignment
which contains homework assignments.   *It is also*
box" ~~where you can know about your homeworks~~. ~~Also is~~ ∧ possible
                                         do
to access ~~to~~ the university library to ~~make~~ resear~~ch~~es~~~~.
                      the
Computers also give students ∧ opportunity to gather information~~s~~
                s   *I*   *This*   *the*
about various topic~~s~~ from the ~~i~~nternet. ~~It~~ is one of ~~most~~
              for students to do
easiest ways ∧ ~~of making~~ research ~~for student~~. One other way

that computers can help students, especially those from ~~an~~other
        to allow students to stay in   *friends*
countries, is ∧ ~~to stay~~ touch with their ~~freinds~~ and family at
               . P   *the USA   I were in*
~~their~~ home~~,~~ ~~p~~ersonally I could not study in ~~usa~~ if ∧ not ∧ con-
                                      a   *and*
tact with my family, because I am both ∧ student ~~as well as~~ ~~work as~~
            family's   *in*
a manager in my ~~families~~ business so I must stay ∧ touch with my
assistants
~~assistents~~.

Paragraph 3

                                      books I have read
One of the most interesting ~~book I am reading~~ recently was a
              W   C   H   the
biography of ~~w~~inston ~~c~~hurchill. ~~h~~e was ∧ prime minister of ~~the~~
       B   *W   W   O*   *people*
Great ~~b~~ritain during ~~the~~ ~~w~~orld ~~w~~ar II. ~~o~~f course many ~~peopel~~
                leader   *B*
know what a great ~~leadership~~ he was during the war. ~~b~~ut I found
                          was
his life before and after the war ~~were~~ also very interesting.

Paragraph 4

Some people ~~are believing~~ *believe* that ^*it* is impossible ~~falling~~ *to fall* in love

with someone "at first sight." ~~In~~ *On* the other hand, there are

~~others~~ *other* people who ~~is believing~~ *believe* that you ~~recognition~~ *recognize* a person

that you love immediately. I know ~~its~~ *it's* possible ~~falling~~ *to fall* in love

at first sight ~~B~~*b*ecause this happened to my wife and ~~I~~ *me*.

Paragraph 5

If you are ever in *T*hailand in ^*the* month of ~~m~~*M*ay I suggest you

~~to~~ go to the Rocket Festival. It ^*is* held every year in a small

town called *Y*~~y~~asothon about 300 ~~mile~~ *miles* from *B*~~b~~angkok. ~~bangkok has~~

~~many beautiful temples, including the temple of the dawn.~~* This

festival is well known ~~and famous~~ in Thailand. People from all

over the country join the local people in ~~celebrate~~ *celebrating*. The local

farmers launch ~~hundred~~ *hundreds* of colorful rockets ~~for gaining~~ *to gain* the

favor of spirits ^*whom* they believe will bring rain to their rice

crops. However, if you go, you need ~~being~~ *to be* careful. Both farmers

~~or~~ *and* tourists ~~sometime~~ *are sometimes* ~~injure~~ *injured* or even ~~kill~~ *killed* by rockets that ~~goes~~ *go*

out of control.

---

*This whole sentence is irrelevant to the paragraph.

Paragraph 6

When I was *a* child I ~~live~~ *lived* in the town of Sendai, the biggest city in the ~~north~~ *northern* part of Japan. My grandmother ~~live~~ *lived* in Tokyo, *W*~~W~~hich is in the ~~center~~ *central* part of ~~J~~*J*apan. While I was ~~live~~ *living* in Sendai, I often went to see my grandmother, but it ~~takes~~ *took* five hours to get to *T*~~t~~okyo by local train. ~~Since~~ *In* 1983, the high-speed express train called the "Shinkansen" *was* built, and connected ~~between~~ Sendai and Tokyo. For me personally, this was *the* most ~~important~~ *important* development in transportation. It now takes only *an* hour and *a* half to travel to Tokyo from Sendai. The trip ~~become~~ *became* very easy. It also ~~was~~ *had* a great impact on Sendai. ~~Economics~~ *Economic* development there increased. ~~In~~ *On* the negative side, prices for housing and other things went up. ~~In~~ *On* the whole, however, this development was very ~~big benefit~~ *beneficial* for the city.

Paragraph 7

I'm from Korea. Once, Koreans had large families. ~~They~~ *Three generations* lived ~~three times families~~ *al*together (grandparents-parents-children). They were almost *all* farmers, so they preferred large numbers of ~~families~~ *children*. ~~In present~~ *Today*, Korea has ~~develop~~ *developed* and society ~~change~~ *has changed* from ~~agriculture~~ *agricultural* to industrial. Many people ~~has~~ *have* moved from rural areas to urban ones~~.~~ ~~B~~*b*ecause *of* their ~~job~~ *jobs* in ~~the city~~ *cities*.

For example, my husband went to Seoul in 1994 ~~for his~~ *to attend* college. He ~~leaved~~ *left* his parents and lived alone. After ~~his~~ graduation, he got a job ~~at~~ *in* Seoul. At that time we worked together. After we ~~marriaged~~ *married*, we lived ~~at~~ *in* Seoul. Of course, his parents ~~want~~ *wanted* us to live ~~together~~ *with* them as Koreans ~~traditional~~ *traditionally* do, but ~~we have~~ *there were* no jobs in ~~parents~~ *their* area. For me ~~personal~~ *personally*, I think ~~this~~ *these* changes ~~of~~ *in* society are natural and reasonable.

Paragraph 8

When I first ~~come~~ *came* to the ~~u~~*U*nited ~~s~~*S*tates I was only 17 years old and ~~have~~ *had* never been away from home. I ~~come~~ *came* here for one year. I lived with ~~a family american~~ *an American family* in a ~~suburban~~ *suburb* of ~~n~~*N*ew ~~o~~*O*rleans, ~~l~~*L*ouisiana. I went to high school there. Imagine how difficult it ~~is~~ *was* for me on ~~a~~ *the* first day of school. I didn't know where ~~should I~~ *I should* go or what ~~should I~~ *I should* do. I ~~spoken~~ *spoke* only *a* little ~~e~~*E*nglish. However, I was very fortunate. The daughter of my host ~~families~~ *family's* neighbors ~~recognizing~~ *recognized* me, and she did everything ~~for~~ *to* ~~helping~~ *help* me. Not only ~~she helped~~ *did she help* me talk with the principal of the school ~~and~~ *but* she *also* introduced me *to* my teacher for the first class. She even ~~eat~~ *ate* lunch with me. I ~~am~~ still ~~remembering~~ *remember* her great kindness!

Exercise 42.2

Answers will vary.

Practice Tests

Practice Test 1

Section 1: Listening
Answer Key
Part A

1. She must live somewhere else.

2. She can use the phone if she wants.

3. Disapproved of Lillian's plan.

4. She cleaned up after cooking.

5. Her father taught her.

6. When the paper is due.

7. There is some classical music she doesn't like.

8. He left some questions unanswered on it.

9. She paid very little for it.

10. The weather hasn't been pleasant until today.

11. Gary can keep her tape player.

12. She originally supported Margaret Ling.

13. Get her own computer.

14. She seems to be feeling better.

15. She needed to prepare for an exam.

Part B

16. They both have the same teacher.

17. In the afternoon.

18. The tools used by ancient people.

19. Airships of the past, present, and future.

20. (C), (A), (B)

21. It flew over the North Pole.

22. The age of large airships ended in disaster there.

23. They would be safer than the rigid airships of the past. / They would use less fuel than modern jet airliners.

24. Reading his work aloud.

25. A novel.

26. The experiences of commercial fishers.

27. (D), (A), (B)

28. Greenland. / Antarctica.

29. (B), (C), (A)

30. They are melting faster than they add new ice.

31. (A)

32. (C)

33. The history of daylight saving time.

34. In the fall.

35. As ridiculous.

36. During World War I.

37. Farmers. / Parents of small children.

38. To help standardize daylight saving time.

Audio Script

Part A

1. **F1:** Excuse me—do you know which apartment Sally Hill lives in?
    M1: Sally Hill? As far as I know, she doesn't live in this apartment complex at all.
    M2: What does the woman imply about Sally Hill?

2. **F2:** Mary, may I use your phone? I think mine is out of order.
    F1: Feel free.
    M2: What does Mary tell the woman?

3. **F1:** Is Lillian still planning to study overseas?
    M1: No, her parents threw cold water on that plan.
    M2: What did Lillian's parents do?

4. **M1:** Uh, oh. Your roommate's making dinner again. Your kitchen is going to look like a tornado hit it.
    F1: Maybe not. Last night she cooked dinner and left the kitchen spick-and-span.
    M2: What does the woman say her roommate did last night?

5. **F1:** That's a beautiful old oak tree over there, but it needs to be sprayed—it has a parasite, I think.

   F2: How did you learn so much about trees?

   F1: Mostly from my father—he studied forestry in college.

   M2: How did the woman mainly learn about trees?

6. (Ring . . . Ring . . . *Sound of phone being picked up*)

   M1: Hello.

   F2: Hi, Tom, this is Brenda. Since you didn't go to class today, I just thought I'd call to tell you that Professor Barclay said we're going to have to write a research paper for his class.

   M1: Really? And how long do we have to finish it?

   M2: What does Tom ask Brenda?

7. **M1:** Julie certainly seems to like classical music.

   F2: She doesn't like just *any* classical music.

   M2: What does the woman imply about Julie?

8. **F1:** How did you do on Professor Dixon's history test?

   M1: Probably not too well. I skipped a couple of questions and I didn't have time to go back to them.

   M2: What does the man say about the history test?

9. **F2:** How do you like this desk I just bought?

   M1: It's beautiful. It must be an expensive antique.

   F2: It may look like that, but I got it for next to nothing.

   M2: What does the woman say about the desk?

10. **M1:** Hi, Emma. On your way home?

    F1: I wish I were. I still have two more classes today. I'd much rather be out there enjoying the sunshine.

    M1: Yeah, it's nice for a change, isn't it?

    M2: What can be inferred from the conversation?

11. **M1:** Gary's using that old tape player of yours.

    F2: He's welcome to it.

    M2: What does the woman mean?

12. **F2:** Who are you going to vote for to be president of the Student Assembly?

    M1: I think Ed Miller is the best choice.

    F2: So do I—now that Margaret Ling has dropped out of the race.

    M2: What does the woman mean?

13. **F1:** I'm going to Stephanie's house. I have an assignment to complete, and I need to use her computer.

    M1: Why don't you buy one of your own? Think how much time you could save.

    M2: What does the man suggest the woman do?

14. **M1:** I just ran into Shelly at the Recreation Center—she said to say hello to you.

   F2: How is she? The last time I spoke to her, she said she hadn't been feeling too well.

   M1: Well, when I saw her this morning, she was the picture of health.

   M2: What does the man say about Shelly?

15. **F1:** I'm really excited about going camping this weekend.

   M1: You're going camping? Then you don't have to study for that physics test after all?

   M2: What had the man originally assumed about the woman?

Audio Script

Part B

Questions 16–18

   F1: Walter, I know you signed up for Professor Crosley's anthropology class. Why haven't you been coming?

   M1: What do you mean? I've been there every morning!

   F1: Every morning? I don't understand. Oh, I get it—you must be in her morning class in cultural anthropology. I'm in her afternoon class in social anthropology. So tell me, how do you like the class?

   M1: Oh, it's pretty interesting. So far, we've been studying the art, the architecture, and the tools of different cultures. And Saturday, our class is going down to the local museum. There's going to be an exhibit of the artifacts of the early inhabitants of this area.

   F1: Your class has quite a different focus from mine. We're studying social relations in groups. For example, this week we've been talking about marriage customs and family life in lots of societies—including our own.

16. What do the two speakers have in common?

17. When does the woman's class meet?

18. Which of the following topics would most likely be discussed in the man's class?

Questions 19–23

   M2: Listen to part of a lecture in an engineering class. The class has been discussing various types of aircraft.

   M1: How many of you were at the football game Saturday night? Did you notice the blimp circling the stadium? That was the blimp *Columbia*. Today's blimps are much smaller descendants of the giant airships that were used in the early twentieth century.
       There are really three types of airships. All of them are lighter-than-air balloons that use engines for power and rudders for steering. Rigid airships contained a number of envelopes or gas cells full of hydrogen. Their shape was determined by a rigid framework of wood or metal. The first rigid airships were flown in Germany by Count Zeppelin in the early 1900s, so they are sometimes called zeppelins. They were used in military operations in World War I. Afterwards, they were used to transport passengers, even taking them across the Atlantic. Another type was the semi-rigid airship,

developed in the 1920s. They looked much like rigid airships, but their shape was maintained by a combination of gas cells and a longitudinal frame made of metal. They were also used for passenger service, military operations, and exploration. The Italian semi-rigid *Norge* was the first airship to fly over the North Pole. Non-rigids were the last type of airship to be developed, and the only kind still flying. They are much smaller than the other two types, and their shape is maintained only by the pressure of gas inside the balloon. They are also much safer because they use helium instead of hydrogen, which burns very easily. They are sometimes called blimps. The blimp *Columbia*, which was flying over the football stadium Saturday night, is non-rigid.

As you may know, the era of the large airships came to an end in Lakehurst, New Jersey in 1937. The famous German rigid airship, *Hindenburg*, full of hydrogen, caught fire and exploded while on a trip to the United States. After that, only a few non-rigid blimps such as the Columbia have been built. They are mainly used for advertising, aerial photography, and sight-seeing trips.

Some engineers, though, hope that large rigid airships will someday fly again. These airships of the future would be equipped with jet engines and filled with helium. They could be used to transport either passengers or cargo. They would not be as fast as today's jet airplanes, but they would be much more fuel-efficient.

19. What is the main subject of the lecture?

20. Match the type of airship with the category in which it belongs.

21. What does the speaker say about the Italian airship *Norge*?

22. What event in the history of airships took place in Lakehurst, New Jersey in 1937?

23. What can be inferred about airships of the future?

Questions 24–26

M2: Listen to a conversation between two students.

F1: Hi, Ted. I just read in the campus paper that your creative writing class is going to be giving a public reading Friday.

M1: Yes, in the ballroom at the Student Union building.

F1: Are you going to be reading some of your poems? You know, I love that poem you wrote about growing up in Alaska.

M1:: Thanks. No, I haven't been writing poetry lately. I've been working on a novel, so I'll read from that on Friday.

F1: A novel? What's it about?

M1: It's about working on a commercial fishing boat.

F1: Really? Do you know much about that?

M1: Well, my grandfather owned a fishing boat, and when I was in high school, I worked on it during the summers. And he told me a million stories about fishing. Of course, I've changed the stories somewhat and fictionalized all the characters for my novel.

F1: Wow, that sounds like it might be an interesting book. Well, I'll try to be there on Friday for the reading.

24. What will Ted be doing on Friday?

25. What has Ted been writing most recently?

26. What is the subject of Ted's most recent writing?

Questions 27–32

M2: Listen to part of a lecture in a geology class.

M1: Good morning, class. As I said at the end of Wednesday's class, today we're going to talk about glaciers. Glaciers begin with ordinary snow. Normal snow is about 80% air space and about 20% solids. Now, when snow doesn't melt, it compacts. Much of the air space disappears, and the snow becomes granular ice called *firn*. Then, as the glacier becomes larger, deeply buried ice becomes even more compressed-about 90% solid-and becomes glacial ice. As the pressure from the weight of accumulated ice builds, the ice on the underside of the glacier becomes pliable enough to flow—usually only a few centimeters a day—and a glacier is born.

There are three main types: valley glaciers, piedmont glaciers, and continental glaciers. Valley glaciers are small glaciers that are confined to a mountain valley. Piedmont glaciers are formed where one or more flow out of their valleys and join together. Continental glaciers are giant, thick, slow-moving sheets of ice. Today, there are only two continental glaciers, one in Antarctica, one in Greenland, but during the Ice Ages, continental glaciers covered most of the northern hemisphere. By definition, continental glaciers cover at least 10,000 square kilometers. The average continental glacier was about the size of the entire state of West Virginia.

At some point, glaciers become stationary. In other words, they appear to stop moving. That's because they are melting at the same rate at which new ice is being added. Then they begin to recede. When they recede, glaciers actually appear to be moving uphill. However, what's really happening is that they are melting faster than they are adding new material.

Because glaciers are so heavy, they can cause large-scale erosion and create interesting features in the process. I'll just mention a couple of those for now. One is called a *cirque*, which is an amphitheater-shaped hollow, carved out of a mountainside. When a single mountain has cirques on at least three of its sides, the peak of the mountain takes on the shape of a pyramid. This peak is called a *horn*. I'll talk about some of the other features glaciers create in a minute, but first, anyone have any questions about glaciers so far?

27. The speaker mentions three types of materials that make up glaciers. Give the order in which these materials appear.

28. Where can continental glaciers be found today?

29. Match the type of glacier with its description.

30. What does the speaker say about receding glaciers?

31. Which part of the picture represents a *cirque*?

32. Which part of the picture represents a *horn*?

Questions 33–38

M2: Listen to a discussion that takes place in a history class.

F1: Well, we have only a few more minutes of class left today. Be sure to read Chapter 8 about the causes of the Civil War for Monday. Oh, and don't forget: On Saturday night, reset your clocks or you'll be an hour late for class on Monday.

F2: Oh, that's right—daylight saving time starts this weekend, doesn't it?

M1: I always forget—do we turn our clocks backwards or forwards?

F2: Don't you know that little saying: spring forward, fall back?

F1: That's right, Linda—in April, we move our clocks forward an hour from standard time to daylight saving time. We reverse that in October, when we turn the clock back an hour to standard time.

M1: So where did the idea of daylight saving time come from anyway, Professor?

F1: Apparently, the first person to propose the idea was Benjamin Franklin, way back in the 1790s. At the time, it was such a novel idea that people thought he was just joking.

F2: When was it put into effect, then?

F1: Not for many years. During World War I, people realized what an innovative idea old Ben Franklin had had. The Sun comes up earlier in the spring and summer, of course, so by moving the clock up then, people can take advantage of the extra daylight.

M1: But what's the real advantage of doing this?

F2: I think I know. You don't need as much fuel for lighting and so on. It's a way to save energy, right, Professor?

F1: Exactly . . . and energy is an important resource, especially during wartime. So the United States first adopted daylight saving time during World War I and went back to it during World War II.

F2: So, we've had daylight saving time since World War II?

F1: Well, not exactly. After the war, some parts of the country went back to year-round standard times and some parts didn't. There were some groups that opposed daylight saving . . .

M1: Really? Who would be against it? It's so nice to have extra daylight in the evening.

F1: Well, anyone who wants more daylight in the morning . . .

F2: Farmers would like that, I suppose, since they get up early to work . . .

F1: Yes, farmers, and some parents who didn't want their children going to school in the dark. Anyway, things were pretty confusing until Congress passed the Uniform Time Act in 1966. That made daylight saving a federal law and standardized the process. Then in 1986, daylight saving time was lengthened by a few weeks, and some people have proposed that we go to a year-round daylight saving time.

33. What is the main topic of this discussion?

34. When are clocks in the United States set *back*?

35. According to the professor, how would most people probably have characterized Benjamin Franklin's plan for daylight saving time when it was first proposed?

36. When was daylight saving time first actually put into effect?

37. Which of these groups opposed daylight saving time?

38. What was the effect of the Uniform Time Act of 1966?

Section 2: Structure
Answer Key and Explanations

Answer	Explanation
1. All	The noun phrase *All team sports* provides a subject for the sentence.
2. <u>light</u>	In order to be parallel with the other adjectives in the series (*harder* and *more resistant*) the comparative form *lighter* must be used.
3. <u>most largest</u>	The correct superlative form is *largest*.
4. a	Of the four choices, only this one, which forms an appositive noun phrase, can correctly complete the sentence.
5. <u>destruction</u>	The adjective form *destructive* is required in place of the noun.
6. <u>which across</u>	The correct word order is preposition + relative pronoun: *across which*.
7. <u>were</u>	The singular form of the verb (*was*) should be used to agree with the singular subject *influence*.
8. without	This is the only correct negative form.
9. Through her research	A preposition (*Through*) is needed before the series of noun phrases that come before the subject. The third choice is incorrect because it lacks the word *her* which is needed for parallelism and because the noun *research* is more appropriate in this series than the gerund *researching*.
10. <u>they are</u>	The pronoun subject *they* is used unnecessarily and should be omitted.
11. <u>when</u>	The relative word *where* must be used to refer to a place.
12. Wherever people	An adverb clause is needed to correctly complete the sentence; only this choice supplies an adverb clause marker and subject.
13. <u>its</u>	In order to agree with a plural noun (*sharks*), the plural possessive word *their* should be used.
14. <u>enough dense</u>	The correct word order is adjective + *enough*: *dense* enough.
15. <u>so</u>	*Such . . . that* is used with an adjective + noun phrase (*different surgical skills*). (*So . . . that* is used when an adjective appears alone.)
16. <u>able</u>	The noun *ability* is needed in place of the adjective.
17. many of which	The correct pattern is quantifier + *of* + relative pronoun.
18. That all	A noun clause, which serves as the subject of the sentence, is required to complete the sentence correctly.

Answer	Explanation
19. <u>chemists</u>	To be parallel with the other nouns in the series (*physics* and *mathematics*), a noun that refers to the name of a field (*chemistry*) is needed.
20. <u>experts</u>	The adjective *expert* should not be pluralized.
21. When	The only correct choice forms a reduced adverb clause.
22. <u>to</u>	The preposition *for* must be used with the adjective *responsible* in this sentence (*responsible* to is sometimes used with a person).
23. are spotted turtles	When a sentence begins with a negative adverbial (*Rarely*), the subject and verb must be inverted.
24. more energy it has	This is a proportional statement; it follows the pattern *The more* X, *the more* Y . . .
25. <u>them</u>	Both the noun phrase (*these craftsmen*) and the pronoun refer to the same persons, so the reflexive pronoun *themselves* should be used.

Reading

1. To describe changes that the Sun will go through

   The primary purpose of this passage is to detail the stages of the Sun's life in the future.

2. The word fueled is closest in meaning to *powered*.

3. The word They refers to **thermonuclear reactions**.

4. The Sun today is a yellow dwarf star. ■ It has existed in its present state for about 4 billion, 600 million years and is thousands of times larger than the Earth. ■ The Sun is fueled by thermonuclear reactions near its center that convert hydrogen to helium. ■ They release so much energy that the Sun can shine for about 10 billion years with little change in its size or brightness. **It maintains its size because the heat deep inside the Sun produces pressure that offsets the force of gravity.** ■ This balance of forces keeps the gases of the Sun from pulling any closer together.

   The last sentence of the paragraph refers to a balance of forces. The missing sentence discusses this balance of forces (between heat and gravity), so it should be placed in front of the last sentence.

5. is approximately halfway through its life as a yellow dwarf

   The Sun has existed in its present state for about 4 billion, 600 million years and can shine for about 10 billion years (paragraph 1). It is expected to become a red giant in about 5 billion years (paragraph 2). Therefore, it is about halfway through its life as a yellow dwarf.

6. The word core is most nearly opposite in meaning to **surface**.

7. The core will grow smaller and hotter.

   Paragraph 2 states that "the core of the Sun will shrink and become hotter."

8. It will become too hot for life to exist.

   The second paragraph describes the process by which the Sun becomes a red giant star. The last sentence of that paragraph states: "Temperatures on the Earth will become too hot for life to exist."

9. thousands of times smaller than it is today

   Paragraph 3 indicates that the Sun will be a white dwarf "after it shrinks to about the size of the Earth." Paragraph 1 indicates that the Sun today is thousands of times larger than the Earth.

   Therefore, the Sun will be thousands of times smaller than it is today.

10. Yellow dwarf, red giant, white dwarf, black dwarf

    According to the passage, the Sun is now a yellow dwarf star; it will then expand to a red giant star, shrink to a white dwarf star, and finally cool to a black dwarf star.

11. The phrase throw off is closest in meaning to *eject*.

12. The word there refers to *the Earth*.

13. Objective

    Although the passage describes the end of the Earth, that event is so far in the future that the author's tone is scientifically dispassionate.

14. He was involved in pioneering efforts to build canals.

    Washington was one of the first people to realize the importance of canals and headed the first company in the United States formed to build a canal.

15. The word feasibility is closest in meaning to *possibility*.

16. The word means is closest in meaning to the word **method**.

17. Hudson River and Lake Erie

    According to paragraph 2, the canal linked Albany on the Hudson River with Buffalo on Lake Erie.

18. The phrase halted is closest in meaning to the phrase **put an end to**.

19. The phrase on-again-off-again is closest in meaning to the word *Intermittent*.

20. the state of New York

    According to the passage, the governor of New York "persuaded the state to finance and build the canal" (paragraph 3).

21. seven million dollars

    The cost had been estimated at $5 million but actually cost $2 million more (paragraph 3), a total of $7 million.

22. The word tolls is closest in meaning to the word *Fees*.

23. It established Boston and Philadelphia as the most important centers of trade.

    According to paragraph 4, the canal "allowed New York to supplant (replace) Boston, Philadelphia, and other eastern cities as the chief center of both domestic and foreign commerce." The other effects are mentioned in this paragraph.

24. They had begun to compete with the Erie Canal for traffic.

    Paragraph 5 indicates that the expansion of the canal would have been warranted "had it not been for the development of the railroads." (This means, "if the railroads had not been developed.") The railroads must have taken so much traffic away from the canal that expansion was no longer needed.

25. The word warranted is closest in meaning to *justified*.

26. The sounds made by trees

    The passage mainly deals with the distress signals of trees. There is no direct information about the other choices in the passage.

27. The reference is to the word *trees* in the third sentence.

28. The word drawn is closest in meaning to **attracted**.

    The word drawn is the past participle of the verb *draw*, which sometimes means *pull* or *attract*.

29. The word parched has the same meaning as **drought-stricken**.

    A *drought* is a time of no rainfall. *Drought-stricken* therefore means damaged by a lack of water. The word *parched* means very dry.

30. The word plight is closest in meaning to *condition*.

    A *plight* is a dangerous or terrible condition.

31. <u>They fastened electronic sensors to the bark of drought-stricken trees and clearly heard distress calls.</u>

32. cannot be heard by the unaided human ear

    The trees' signals are in the 50–500 kilohertz range; the unaided human ear can detect no more than 20 kilohertz (paragraph 2).

33. The word fractured is closest in meaning to **cracked**.

34. Lack of water

    The signals are caused when the water column inside tubes in trees break, "a result of too little water."

35. The word they refers to **insects**.

36. In the context of the passage, pick up means *Perceive*.

37. changes in color

    The first and second choice are mentioned in paragraph 3; the third choice is mentioned throughout the passage; there is no mention of the fourth choice.

38. was continuing

    Paragraph 3 says, "Researchers are now running tests," implying that, at the time the article was written, research was continuing.

39. analyze an important film

    The purpose of the passage is primarily to describe Charlie Chaplin's movie, *Modern Times*.

40. a conversation with a reporter

Paragraph 1 states that Chaplin "was motivated to make the film by a reporter" during an interview.

41. The word jammed is closest in meaning to *packed*.

42. takes place outside a factory

According to paragraph 3, "Scenes of factory interiors account for only about one-third of the footage." Therefore, about two-thirds of the film must have been shot outside the factory.

43. The word biting is most nearly opposite in meaning to the word *gentle*. (*Biting* here means "sharply critical.")

44. The phrase *going insane* could best replace the phrase losing his mind .

45. Scenes of factory interiors account for only about one-third of the footage of *Modern Times*, but they contain some of the most pointed social commentary as well as the funniest comic situations. ■ No one who has seen the film can ever forget Chaplin vainly trying to keep pace with the fast-moving conveyor belt, almost losing his mind in the process. ■ Another popular scene features an automatic feeding machine brought to the assembly line so that workers need not interrupt their labor to eat. **All at once, this feeding device begins to malfunction.** ■ It hurls food at Chaplin, who is strapped into his position on the assembly line and cannot escape. ■ This serves to illustrate people's utter helplessness in the face of machines that are meant to serve their basic needs.

The word It in the sentence following the missing sentence refers to the feeding device. Also, this sentence describes the malfunction that is first mentioned in the missing sentence.

46. The word their refers to *people's*.

47. helplessness

The last sentence of paragraph 3 states: "This (the scene) serves to illustrate people's utter helplessness in the face of machines that are meant to serve their basic needs."

48. The word utter is closest in meaning to *complete*.

49. The word faults is closest in meaning to **flaws**.

50. revolutionary

The film "does not offer a radical social message" (Paragraph 3) and so would not be considered "revolutionary." Paragraph 2 states that "Chaplin preferred to entertain rather than lecture" so it is "entertaining." Paragraph 3 mentions that people who have seen the film cannot forget certain scenes, so it is certainly "memorable." According to paragraph 2, the opening scene's "biting tone . . . is replaced by a gentle note of satire;" therefore, the author would consider the film "satirical."

Practice Test 2

Section 1: Listening
Answer Key
Part A

1. Only four of them are expensive.

2. Nearly all of the students can meet then.

3. He intends to see Michelle.

4. Through his sister.

5. It's not easy to find inexpensive housing near campus.

6. He's not taking as many classes this term.

7. They were impolite.

8. He doesn't have to hurry.

9. It was much too loud.

10. It was unexpectedly busy.

11. The lab is generally locked on Saturdays.

12. She did well on the test.

13. They are not new students.

14. His picture hadn't been taken.

15. Not many people go there at this time of year.

16. He needs the insurance no matter how much it costs.

Part B

17. A roommate.

18. Her phone number.

19. $30.

20. A slide projector./Acrylic paints.

21. (D)

22. They are extremely lifelike.

23. Write down their reactions to the slides.

24. The stages of children's language learning.

25. (B), (A), (C)

26. Between two and three years.

27. They are quite logical.

28. The class hasn't had a chance to read about them.

29. Professor Kim.

30. Economics.

31. Time to work on research.

32. He and Emily Dickinson were influential poets.

33. For her unusual habits.

34. Their economy.

35. (D), (B), (C), (A)

36. 1,700.

Audio Script

Part A

1. **M2:** Have you seen the book list for Professor McKnight's class? We have to buy eight books. That's going to cost a fortune.
   F1: But four of them are paperbacks. Those aren't very expensive.
   F2: What does the woman imply about the books?

2. **F1:** Can everyone in the class meet in the library on Friday?
   M1: Everyone but Lisa.
   F2: What does the man mean?

3. **M2:** My sociology seminar was canceled for today.
   F1: So, Rob, what are you going to do with your free afternoon?
   M2: I thought I'd pay Michelle a visit.
   F2: What does Rob mean?

4. **F1:** Who was that woman you were talking to at the reception?
   M1: That's Carol Donovan. She was my sister's roommate in college.
   F2: How is the man acquainted with Carol Donovan?

5. **M1:** It's getting harder and harder to find affordable housing near campus.
   F1: Isn't it though!
   F2: What does the woman mean?

6. **F1:** What classes are you taking this term, Rick?
   M1: Same as last term, only I'm not taking history.
   F2: What does Rick mean?

7. **M2:** I meant to ask you—what did you think of David's comments to the teacher?
    F1: Kind of rude, weren't they?
    F2: What was the woman's opinion of David's comments?

8. **M1:** I need a few more minutes to fill out this form.
    F1: Take your time.
    F2: What does the woman tell the man?

9. **F1:** Matthew, do you think the music was too loud?
    M2: Well, no—not if you wanted the people across town to hear it!
    F2: What does Matthew imply about the music?

10. **F1:** This was *supposed* to be a quiet, relaxing weekend.
    M2: But it didn't quite turn out that way, did it?
    F2: What does the man imply about the weekend?

11. **F1:** The front door to the lab was unlocked on Saturday morning.
    M1: Really? That's strange.
    F2: What can be inferred from this conversation?

12. **F1:** Did Morgan pass the test?
    M2: Pass it? With flying colors!
    F2: What does the man say about Morgan?

13. **F1:** This schedule says we have to attend an orientation session before we can register.
    M2: That's just for new students.
    F2: What can be inferred about these two speakers?

14. **F1:** You look great in this picture, Larry. Look how you're smiling!
    M1: So you *did* take that picture of me after all!
    F2: What had Larry *originally* assumed?

15. **F1:** I need to get away for the weekend to somewhere peaceful and quiet.
    M2: Why don't you go down to Gold Beach? It's very quiet there at this time of year.
    F1: It would cost too much to stay there.
    M2: Not now. During the off-season, hotel rooms are dirt cheap.
    F2: What can be inferred about Gold Beach from the conversation?

16. **M1:** This insurance policy has gotten so expensive, I can hardly afford it anymore.
    F1: But Greg, you can't really afford NOT to have it, can you?
    F2: What does the woman tell Greg?

Audio Script

Part B

Questions 17–19

F2: Listen to the following phone conversation.

(Ring . . . ring . . . ring . . . *sound of phone being picked up*)

M1: Hello, Campus Daily, advertising department.

F1: Hi, I'm calling to place a couple of ads.

M1: Sure. Under what classification?

F1: Well, I want one in the "Roommate Wanted" section.

M1: All right. And how would you like that to read?

F1: Okay, it should read, "Female roommate wanted for pleasant, sunny, two-bedroom apartment on Elliewood Avenue, three blocks from campus. Share rent and utilities. Available September 1. Call between 5 and 9 P.M. Ask for Cecilia."

M1: Okay, fine. And what about your other ad?

F1: That one I'd like under "Merchandise for Sale," and I'd like it to read "Matching blue and white sofa and easy chair, excellent condition, $350 or best offer. Call between 5 and 9 P.M. Ask for Cecilia." Did you get all that?

M1: Uh huh. You'll want your phone number on these, right?

F1: Oh, sure, thanks for reminding me—it's 555-6972. And I'd like the ads to run for a week.

M1: It's five dollars a week per line. Each of your ads will take up three lines, so that's $15 per ad.

17. Which of the following is Cecilia trying to find?

18. Which of the following does Cecilia *initially* forget to tell the man?

19. What is the total amount that the two advertisements will cost for one week?

Questions 20–23

F2: Listen to part of a lecture that takes place in an art history class. The class has been discussing twentieth century art.

M1: Good morning, class. Today we'll continue our study of twentieth century art movements with a discussion of photo realism, a style popular in the 1960s and 1970s. Painters who worked in this style realistically portrayed their subjects down to the smallest detail, and so their paintings resemble photographs in many respects. In fact, many of the painters in this field worked from photographs or slides rather than from life. For example, in a few minutes I'll show you a painting by Audrey Flack called *The Farb Family Portrait*. To paint this picture, she projected a slide of a photo she had taken of the family onto her canvas to guide her painting. She used an airbrush to apply acrylic paints to the canvas. The acrylics account for the bright, luminous colors you'll see in most of her work. Photo realist painters generally chose subjects that were interesting only because they were so ordinary. One photo realist said that his subjects were "so normal that they are shocking." You'll see a closed down gas station, a broken neon sign, an elderly man waiting for a bus, a dilapidated billboard.

Sculptors who worked in this style, such as Duane Hanson, often created life-size sculptures of very ordinary people—construction workers, tourists, police officers, sales clerks, homeless people. Hanson's sculptures are so lifelike that sometimes visitors to a gallery or museum come up to them and ask them questions.

Okay, now I'm going to show you some slides of various works of photo realism. I'd like all of you to take notes while you're viewing these slides, and then over the weekend, I'd like you to write a short paper-just a page or two-that describes your reactions to these works.

20.   Which of the following did Audrey Flack use to paint *Farb Family Portrait*?

21.   Which of the following illustrations would most likely be classified as a work of photo realism?

22.   According to the speaker, why are the works of sculptor Duane Hanson so remarkable?

23.   What does the teacher ask the class to do over the weekend?

Questions 24–28

F2:   Listen to a discussion in a linguistics class.

F1:   Professor Jordan?

M2:   Yes, Grace?

F1:   I know it says on our syllabus that we are going to talk about how children acquire language next week, but I wonder if I could ask you a few questions about this process now?

M2:   Sure. What did you want to know?

F1:   Well, how old are children before they start to actually say words?

F1:   They start making language-like sounds when they are from two to four months old. These noises generally seem to begin with the letters *g* or *k*, because these are the easiest sounds for infants to make.

F1:   My little niece is four months old and she's already saying "mama."

M1:   Really? I didn't know children that young could say any meaningful words.

M2:   To tell you the truth, Grace, your niece is probably just making a noise that sounds like "mama." Between four months and six months, children usually begin to babble meaningless syllables. Most common are those beginning with *p, b, d, m,* or *n* followed by a vowel.

F1:   So, when kids that age say *mama* or *dada*, it's just a coincidence?

M2:   It probably is. Adults often misinterpret these sounds as true words.

M1:   When do children say their first real words?

M2:   Usually when they are between six months and a year. At first, they say single words. At about a year to eighteen months, they begin forming two word combinations, such as "all gone," "more milk," "see doggie."

F1:   Does it make any difference what language the children's parents speak? I mean, if a child's parents speak French or Chinese, do they learn different words first?

M2:   Apparently not. In fact, the one and two-word utterances that children first use are so similar all around the world that they read like translations of one another.

F1: Really? That's amazing!

M1: How fast do kids learn new words?

M2: At first, not very quickly—only a few words a month, but this accelerates rapidly. By the age of two or three, children have learned thousands of words, can form complete sentences and have mastered the basics of grammar. Can you believe it? A two-and-a-half-year old toddler is a grammatical genius, and all without studying a single rule!

F1: Well, true—but kids DO make mistakes when they speak.

M2: Yes, they do, but most of the time their errors are very logical. They are often the result of "overlearning" grammatical patterns. For example, children will say, "I saw two mans" because they over-learned the rule for forming plurals, or they'll say "We goed to Gramma's house" because they overlearned the rule for forming the past tense.

M1: But what I don't understand is how this all happens. I mean, how does a child that age learn such a complex thing as language. I've been studying German since high school, and I don't speak it nearly as well as a two-year-old German child.

M2: Well, language acquisition is a somewhat mysterious process, and there are several conflicting theories about it. Some of these are presented in Chapter 8 in your textbook. Before we discuss them, though, I want you to have read that chapter.

24. What is the main topic of this discussion?

25. The professor discusses sounds, words, and phrases that children use at certain ages. Match the sound or phrase with the age at which a typical child would first begin to use it.

26. At what age do most children begin to master the basics of grammar?

27. What does Professor Jordan say about the grammatical mistakes that two- and three-year-olds make?

28. Why does Professor Jordan not discuss the theories about how children acquire language?

Questions 29–31

F2: Listen to a conversation between two students.

F1: Paul, I tried to call you last night. Were you at the library?

M2:: No, I went to the academic awards ceremony.

F1: Oh, who won the Outstanding Faculty Award this year? Was it Professor Kim from the biology department again?

M2: No, there's a rule that says you can't win it more than one year in a row. This year Professor Callahan won.

F1: I've heard of her, but I've never taken any classes from her.

M2: I have. I took a course in micro from her last semester. She's really a good teacher, but she works her students pretty hard.

F1: What did she do to win that award?

M2: Well, Chancellor Davis, who presented the award, said Professor Callahan has published several papers on historical economics and that she and her colleague Professor Woods got a research grant from the government to generate computer models of the economy. And she always got top evaluations from her students.

F1: So what did she win? Cash?

M2: No, but she'll be able to take a term off from teaching at full salary to work on any research project that she likes.

29. Who won the Outstanding Faculty Award *last* year?

30. In what department does Professor Callahan probably teach?

31. What prize did Professor Callahan receive?

Questions 32–36

F2: Listen to a lecture in an American literature class. The class has been discussing nineteenth century American poetry.

M1: Good morning, class. In our last class, we talked about Walt Whitman, and said he was one of the two great voices of American poetry in the nineteenth century. The other was Emily Dickinson. Their poetry could not have been more different. Dickinson claimed that she never even read Whitman's poems. And their lifestyles could not have been more different. But they were both important innovators. I said before that Whitman became well-known around the world. Dickinson was famous only in her own village—Amherst, Massachusetts—and that was not for her poetry but for her mysterious ways. You see, she almost never left the house of her father, who was a wealthy lawyer. When she did appear in public, she always wore white dresses like a bride. While this may not seem too strange to us today, it was pretty unusual behavior for Amherst in the 1800s!

For a woman who lived such an uneventful life, though, she wrote amazingly perceptive poems about nature, love, and death. Her poems are all short and untitled. What I particularly admire about these poems is their economy—she was able to say so much in so few words! She was a very prolific writer. In one year alone, 1874, the year her father died, she wrote over 200 poems. But she never intended that her poems would be published. At least seven of them were published during her lifetime in newspapers and magazines, but that was against her will. After her death in 1886, her family discovered that she had written over 1,700 poems. Her family arranged to have a collection of about 30 of her poems published a few years later, and eventually, all of them appeared in print. In 1950, Harvard University bought all of her manuscripts and acquired the publishing rights to all her poems. Harvard published a complete three-volume collection of her poems and letters five years later.

Now, we'll take a look at some of her poems, but first . . . questions, anyone?

32. What point does the professor make about Walt Whitman?

33. Why was Emily Dickinson famous in her hometown?

34. What does the professor say that he particularly admires about the poems of Emily Dickinson?

35. The professor mentions several events in the history of the publication of Emily Dickinson's poetry. Put these events in the proper order.

36. About how many of Emily Dickinson's poems were probably included in the collection published by Harvard University?

Section 2: Structure

Answer	Explanation
1. than dull ones	The word *than* is needed to complete the comparison.
2. <u>and</u>	The correct pattern is *either . . . or*.
3. <u>oldest than</u>	The comparative *older* is needed in place of the superlative *oldest*.
4. who became	An adjective (relative) clause is required to complete the sentence.
5. <u>journalist</u>	The noun that names a field (*journalism*) is needed in place of the noun naming a person (*journalist*).
6. an understanding	After a two-word verb (*depends on*), a gerund (*-ing* form) must be used.
7. No	The negative adjective *No* is required before a noun phrase (*single dialect*).
8. <u>market</u>	To be parallel with the other nouns in the series (*agriculture*, *finance*, and *accounting*), a noun that names a field should be used (*marketing*).
9. <u>numbers</u>	Before an uncountable noun (*fuel*), the word *amounts* should be used in place of numbers.
10. <u>are</u>	The singular verb *is* must be used to agree with the singular subject *sum*.
11. Although	An adverb clause marker is needed to complete the sentence.
12. <u>both insulated</u>	Before a series of three elements (*insulated*, *ventilated*, and *equipped*) the conjunction *both* cannot be used.
13. Henry Hobson Richardson designed many of the buildings at Harvard University	The participle phrase at the beginning of the sentence (*Considered one of America's first great architects. . . .*) must refer to a person; only this choice has a person as the subject.
14. <u>another</u>	The word *other* must be used before the plural noun types.
15. <u>too</u>	The correct expression is *so many . . . that*. (*Too* is used in phrases with infinitives: *too many to . . .*)
16. <u>it</u>	The plural pronoun *them* must be used to agree with the plural noun *bridges*.
17. <u>very relatively</u>	The word *very* cannot correctly modify the word *relatively*.
18. allowing them	The present participle *allowing* forms a reduced adjective clause; it really means *which allows them to. . . .*

Answer	Explanation
19. <u>wildly</u>	The adjective *wild* should replace the adverb *wildly* because the phrase modifies a noun (*Magnolia Gardens*). The word *lovely* is used correctly in this sentence because it is an adjective ending in *-ly*, not an adverb.
20. <u>instrument</u>	The plural noun *instruments* is needed here.
21. to be controlled	After a noun modified by *first*, an infinitive is usually used; in this sentence, a passive infinitive (*to* + *be* + past participle) is needed because the action is performed by the board of regents, not by the university.
22. <u>running</u>	This sentence incorrectly compares a sport and people (*running* and *race walkers*). For a logical comparison, the word *running* must be changed to *runners*.
23. <u>age which</u>	The preposition *in* has been omitted: *age in which*.
24. Perhaps	This sentence is correctly introduced by a prepositional phrase that has the meaning of an adverb clause (*because* of *the . . .*); the first and fourth choices are incorrect because they contain verbs. The third choice is incorrect; the word *besides* does not make any sense here.
25. <u>easy</u>	The noun *ease* is needed to be parallel with the noun *difficulty*.

Section 3: Reading

1. Humans and mammoths in the New World
   The passage generally deals with the time humans and mammoths co-existed in the New World, and the possible role humans played in the extinction of the mammoths. No specific details are offered about the first and second choices, and the third is too general.

2. The word remote is most nearly opposite in meaning to ***recent***.

3. The word implements is closest in meaning to *tools*.

4. The phrase these early migrants refers to *humans*.

5. The word reigned is closest in meaning to ***dominated***.

6. In the southern part of North America
   Paragraph 2 mentions "the imperial mammoth of the South," meaning the southern section of North America.

7. had previously hunted mammoths in Siberia

   Paragraph 2 states that "Here, as in the Old World, there is evidence that humans hunted these elephants," implying that humans had also hunted mammoths in Siberia.

8. (C)

9. The word ~~remains~~ is closest in meaning to *bones*.

The word *remains* can be defined as those parts of an animal's body that can be found after many years. In this case, they are mainly the bones of the mammoths.

10. The phrase ~~wiped out~~ is closest in meaning to **doomed**.

11. The cause of their extinction is unknown.

The author argues that the first choice is unlikely. The second choice is not possible because the extinction of the mammoths came at the END of the Ice Age. There is no information about the fourth choice. Only the third choice is a possible conclusion.

12. The word ~~cunning~~ is closest in meaning to *clever*.

13. They were concentrated in a small area.

The first choice is true; paragraph 4 states that humans were "not very numerous." The second choice is true; paragraph 1 states that humans had bows and arrows at the time that they crossed from Siberia. The fourth choice is also true; paragraph 4 states that humans were "cunning hunters." Only the third choice is NOT true; paragraph 4 says that "humans were still widely scattered."

14. The early history of jazz

The passage chiefly deals with the first decades of jazz, the Dixieland era.

15. As used in this sentence, the word ~~idiom~~ means **style**—a style of playing music.

16. New Orleans

According to the first paragraph, the earliest recordings were made by the Original Dixieland Jazz Band, white musicians who "came to Chicago from New Orleans."

17. In 1923

According to paragraph 2, the first important recording made by black musicians was recorded by "King" Oliver's Creole Jazz Band in 1923.

18. "King" Oliver's Creole Jazz Band

Paragraph 2 says that "King" Oliver's Creole Jazz Band "featured some of the foremost jazz musicians of the time, including . . . Louis Armstrong."

19. The piano

Paragraph 3 indicates that the beat was provided by the rhythm section, which included the piano.

20. The word ~~them~~ refers to **his musicians**.

21. used written arrangements

According to paragraph 3, Duke Ellington "provided his musicians with written arrangements."

22. Rigidly planned

Paragraph 3 states that "improvisation was an indispensable element," indicating that Dixieland was NOT rigidly planned. All of the other answer choices are referred to in paragraph 3.

23. All during the 1920s, jazz gained in popularity. ■ In fact, the period itself became known as "the jazz era." All sections of the country were caught up in the music and the dances associated with it. ■ The two most important performance and recording centers were Chicago and New York. ■ The most influential jazz artists in Chicago were members of small bands such as the Wolverines, usually consisting of only four or five musicians. **In New York City, on the other hand, the trend was toward larger groups.** ■ These bands usually contained two trumpets, one or two trombones, three or four reeds, and a five- or six-musician rhythm section. They played in revues, large dance halls, and theaters. ■ Bands would become larger still during the next age of jazz, the Swing era.

The sentence before the missing one describes the small bands of Chicago. The sentence following the missing one describes a large one. The missing sentence introduces the idea that in New York City the bands tended to be large.

24. A small jazz band

Paragraph 4 refers to the Wolverines as an example of a small Chicago jazz band.

25. The author provides the most detailed description of early jazz in paragraph 3.

26. the Swing era

The last sentence of the passage indicates that the next era of jazz would be the Swing era, so it is logical that the next paragraph will continue with a discussion of this period.

27. The word astounding is closest in meaning to *startling*.

28. they have varying amounts of traffic

All three streets are in San Francisco; the residents have the same approximate levels of income. (They are all middle class or working class.) They each have approximately the same ethnic mix as well. The only difference is the amount of traffic.

29. 16,000

Paragraph 1 says that Franklin Street "had around 16,000 cars a day."

30. increased amounts of trash

According to paragraph 2, trash is a secondary effect of heavy traffic.

31. The phrase hardly ever is closest in meaning to *seldom*.

32. The word Many refers to *residents*.

33. Heavy traffic brought with it danger, noise, fumes, and soot, directly, and trash secondarily. ■ That is, the cars didn't bring in much trash, but when trash accumulated, residents seldom picked it up. ■ The cars, Appleyard determined, reduced the amount of territory residents felt responsible for ■ Franklin Street residents hardly ever interacted with their neighbors and went out on the street only when they had some compelling reason to do so. ■ Many covered their doors and windows and spent most of their time in the rear of their houses. **Even so, traffic noise was a constant intrusion into their lives.** ■ Most families with children had already moved elsewhere.

The phrase *Even so* often means that an unsuccessful attempt to do something was made. In this case, it refers to the effort to cope with noise by covering the windows and doors and spending time in the back of the house.

34. Octavia Street

Paragraph 3 deals with how Octavia Street residents interact; they have more friends and acquaintances on their block than Franklin Street residents do, and by implication, than Gough Street residents do as well.

35. The word chatted is closest in meaning to *talked*.

36. "People who live here have more and more space for which they feel responsible."

According to the passage, increased traffic REDUCES the amount of territory for which residents feel responsible. All the other statements would be consistent with information given about Gough Street residents in paragraph 4.

37. HEAVY, LIGHT, MEDIUM

The author supplies details first about Franklin Street (HEAVY), then Octavia Street (LIGHT), and finally Gough Street (MEDIUM).

38. a writer

The passage concentrates on the books written by Rachel Carson and on her career as a writer.

39. Zoology

Paragraph 1 states that Carson studied zoology at Johns Hopkins University.

40. *The Sea Around Us*

Carson won the National Book Award for nonfiction for this book (paragraph 2).

41. sold many copies

According to paragraph 2, when *Under the Sea Wind* was first published "it received excellent reviews, but sales were poor until it was reissued in 1952."

42. The word intriguing is closest in meaning to **fascinating**.

43. A research expedition

There is no mention that Rachel Carson took part in a research expedition. The other sources are given in paragraph 2.

44. Highly technical

Carson "realized the limitations of her non-technical readers" (paragraph 2), implying that the book was not highly technical. It did have a poetic quality, and it was "fascinating" (interesting), and well-researched.

45. The word It refers to the book **Silent Spring**.

46. The word reckless is closest in meaning to *irresponsible*.

47. a warning about the dangers of misusing insecticides

Paragraph 3 states that the book *Silent Spring* "proved how much harm was done by the . . . reckless use of insecticides."

48. In 1962 Carson published *Silent Spring*, which sparked considerable controversy regarding the use of pesticides and which basically led to the formation of the worldwide environmental movement.

49. To support the ideas in *Silent Spring*

Carson's work "was vindicated" by the report (paragraph 3), implying that the report contradicted the chemical industry's claims and supported the ideas in Carson's book *Silent Spring*.

50. To define economic resources

The passage deals with the two main divisions of economic resources: property resources and human resources. The other choices refer to minor details in the passage.

51. the topic of economic resources is a broad one

This expression is used figuratively in the passage to mean that economic resources is a broad topic.

52. is much more restrictive than when economists use it

According to paragraph 2, economists "mean much more than the non-economist" by the term *land*.

53. The word ⬜arable⬜ means "able to be cultivated"—and therefore, *fertile* is closest in meaning to this word.

54. ⬜The latter⬜ (which means the second concept mentioned before; *the former* means the first concept mentioned before) refers to **consumer goods**.

55. A railroad

capital goods include aids to transporting goods (paragraph 2), such as a railroad. Money is specifically mentioned as NOT being a type of capital in paragraph 2. The third choice is an example of land, not of capital, since it is a natural resource. The fourth choice is an example of labor.

56. Production

The author defines *land* and *capital* in paragraph 2 and labor in paragraph 3. Although the author mentions *production*, there is no specific definition of it offered in the passage.

57. The word ⬜heading⬜ is closest in meaning to the word **category**.

58. entrepreneurs

The third paragraph indicates that the term "labor" involves all types of human talents except entrepreneurial skills, which are considered a separate category.

59. The word ⬜infinite⬜ is most nearly opposite in meaning to **limited**.

60. The word ⬜lack⬜ is closest in meaning to **shortage**.